© The Bluecoat Press 2002

Published by The Bluecoat Press, Liverpool
Book design by March Design, Liverpool
Printed by MFP

Back cover photographs from Dorothy Curl's family album

ISBN 1 872568 99 8

Acknowledgments

We feel we must pay tribute to those women who joined the group, made an excellent contribution, then for various reasons left to go on to do other things. However, we must remember very specially, Stella Chambers, a founder member who is not well enough to attend our sessions. It was Stella who made the rag rug, which is the centrepiece of all our scenes. When we were unable to buy wraparound pinafores, Stella made them, as well as snoods, dolls from old socks, and whizzers. She scoured car boot sales and markets for artefacts of yesteryear. She stored them in her home when we had nowhere to keep them, and ferried them to and fro whenever we needed them. Her memories of the 1930s were sharp and clear. She was a very great asset to the group. Many thanks Stella, we could not have done it without you.

Also, our book would not have materialised without the invaluable help of the following: The Nuffield Foundation, The Liverpool Maritime Museum, Dilys Horwich, Colin Shuker, Joan Boyce, Eileen Kelly.

And finally, the many thousands of schoolchildren who attend our workshops and their teachers and parents who bring them, some from as far afield as Leeds, Wales, Warrington, Wigan, Preston and, of course, Merseyside. Their enthusiasm and interest make it all worthwhile.

Thank you so much, we are indebted to you all.

A DIFFERENT WORLD

Memories of life in the 1930s and 1940s

The Liverpool Women's History Group

The Bluecoat Press

The Versatile Age

The old rocking chair is empty today
For Grandmother is no longer in it.
She's off in her car to her office or shop
And buzzes around every minute.
No one shoves Grandma back on the shelf,
She is versatile, forceful, dynamic.
That's not a pie in the oven my dear!
Her baking today is ceramic!
You won't see her trundling off early to bed
From her place in a warm chimney nook,
Her typewriter clicketty-clacks through the night
For Grandma is writing a book.
Grandma ne'er takes a backward look
To slow her steady advancing,
She won't tend the babies for you anymore
For Grandma has taken up dancing.
She is not content with crumbs of old thoughts
With meagre and secondhand knowledge –
Don't bring your mending for Grandma to do
For Grandma has gone back to college!

Anonymous

Contents

The Liverpool Women's History Group

Back row
Mollie Connor, Nina Barr, Barbara Harrison, Margaret McGarry, Ann Roberts, Margaret Gillin, Lil Otty and Lily Jones.
Middle row
Phyl Kenny, Tina Silverston, Deryn Jones, Vera Jeffers and Anne Baker.
Front row
Dorothy Curl and Doris Windsor.

Introduction

We are a group of fourteen elderly women, three of whom are octogenarians, others in their mid to late seventies and the babies of the group, who are between fifty and sixty years old.

We first became acquainted whilst attending a course, 'Second Chance to Learn', at Liverpool Community College. This was a one-year course and at the end of it most of us stayed on to study 'Women's History, Women's Lives', another optional course on Second Chance to Learn. We came to realise that women had been overlooked in history books and we sought to redress the balance somewhat by writing books such as, *Born to Serve, Can You Hear the Heart Beat?, Women on the Waterfront*, etc, which highlight the importance of women's lives.

Later, schools requested that we visit them and tell the children what life was like when we were young. We agreed, but it was difficult travelling on public transport and we had very few artefacts to show the children.

It was suggested that we could use the Maritime Museum for our meetings, rehearsals and workshops, and borrow artefacts such as a large wooden table and chairs, old wireless sets etc. This was a wonderful opportunity. For our workshops to be realistic, we needed scenery. Lily Jones, a friend of the group, painted various backdrops, such as an old fireplace with a lovely warm fire ablaze and the kettle on the hob, a wartime window with strips of brown paper criss-crossed on it, and corner shop scenes, complete with shelves full of the old commodities of yesteryear and a typical shop window. This all helped to set the scene and make our workshops come to life. We have now had thousands of children come to see our workshops, some from as far afield as Wales and Leeds, and many from Wigan, Preston and Warrington. But of course, the majority of them come from Merseyside schools.

The letters of appreciation we receive are legion; every one of them telling us how much they have learnt and what fun they have had. There lies the crunch of the matter, we are teaching the children Social History in a fun way and bridging the gap between young and old.

We meet every Wednesday afternoon at the Education Suite in the Maritime Museum. At the outset we made many mistakes, among them was writing scripts like a play and trying to remember our lines – not easy when you are in your declining years! In desperation we decided at one point to have our script on the table, so that we could refer to it from time to time, until one day someone moved the sugar basin and covered the script. We were stymied! At our next meeting we decided to dispense with a script altogether – we would just talk naturally, as the words came into our heads. Our new, improvised scenes brought about an immediate improvement. Today, we are learning by our mistakes and gradually perfecting our performances.

The women first met on a 'Second Chance to Learn' course at Liverpool Community College. They now meet every Wednesday at Merseyside Maritime Museum and hold regular workshops for schools on life in Liverpool in the 1930s and 40s.

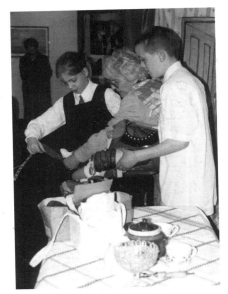

It is most important that the children are encouraged to participate and we include them in the scenes by having them weigh out sugar, pat butter, buy a bundle of chips, be an evacuee, take food to the shelter, or get bathed in front of the fire. They really love this. We are never short of volunteers, and the problem is trying to include all of the children in some capacity. The letters we receive from them are so appreciative and they all say how thrilled they were at having been given a part.

During the workshops we try to involve as many children as possible in every scene and we are never short of volunteers.

We try to introduce as much humour into the workshops as possible, whilst highlighting the hardship and trauma of those years, the Depression in the thirties and the horrors of war. We try to make them laugh and sometimes they cry, and we always sing them in and sing them out.

For ourselves, we have found a direct and enjoyable way of using our personal memories to teach children history, and in doing so, have discovered talents in ourselves which we never knew we had. We have found lasting friendship and mutual support from the group and in our workshops and in our writing, we hope to give the children an insight into a very different world. We feel worthwhile and it has proved very therapeutic, far better than sitting at home feeling sorry for ourselves.

We perform two different workshops: one on the 1930s and the other on the war and the 1940s. Before describing our workshops here is a note from Lily Jones, our Artistic Director:

About ten tears ago, my good pal, Phyl Kenny, asked me if I would paint an old-fashioned, black-leaded grate for the Women's History Group, of which she was a member. The snag was that it had to be life-sized! I took up the challenge and that is how I became involved in the painting of the backdrops for their improvisations at the Maritime Museum.

An artistic streak shows up in my family from time to time, it has come down the line from my dad's maternal grandfather, who bore the splendid

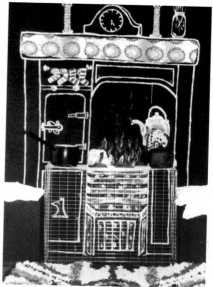

Lily Jones, our resident artist, has painted or sketched backdrops for every scene in both our workshops.

name of Edmund O'Brien, and had travelled from America to Liverpool as an art student. He met his fate in the person of Hannah Dixon, married her and lived and worked in Liverpool for the rest of his life. He is mentioned in the Gores Directory of 1870 as a sculptor. I know he worked on some of the statues of the Walker Art Gallery complex, as a sub-contractor. Where his talent originated, I do not know, but being of Irish descent, I like to think that it was passed from generations of artists, perhaps from an early Celtic nun or monk, who sat for long hours illuminating manuscripts!

I left school at the age of fifteen, worked in a grocer's for a year, and then was fortunate enough to pass the entrance exam for Wallasey School of Art. I spent two years at the Art School and recall that one of the subjects we had to paint was a bunch of rhododendrons. Unfortunately, I left there before obtaining any certificate, simply because I was entirely fed up with never having money except for that earned in a café during holiday breaks. No student grants or loans available then! But no education is ever wasted, and I received a very good grounding in anatomy, sculpture, pottery, painting and perspective, which over the years has given me much pleasure and also a little extra income from the sale of paintings.

Artists see the world differently, taking mental snap-shots of incidents and scenes and continually squirrelling them away in the mind's eye for future use. So that, when asked to do a backdrop of wartime, a corner-shop, evacuation, street parties, or children playing street games, the material is all waiting patiently to pop out as required!

I decided to adopt a cartoon-like style for the back-drops, which seems to have worked quite well and the ladies seem to like it too. Of course I greatly admire all the dedicated hard work and whole-hearted enthusiasm which they put into their wonderful plays, vividly bringing to life our childhood years of hard times, for today's schoolchildren. I also enjoy very much indeed being an honourary member of their group.

1930s Workshop

As the children arrive for the workshop, we welcome them with one of our childhood songs, such as *The Alley, Alleyo,* making an archway with our arms for them to walk under.

The narrator then makes sure that all the children are settled and comfortable and that they can all see and hear properly. Recently we had a party of blind children who, of course, were given seats on the front row. They joined in all the scenes and were given ample opportunity both during and after the performance to handle and in some cases smell the various artefacts. The narrator begins by telling the children that the 1930s were a long time ago, about seventy years, in fact, and that we were children then and have lots of memories of that time.

"We are going to tell you some of our memories, so that you will have some idea about how we lived and the things we did way back then in the thirties. The backdrops that you see here will give you a good idea of what our homes were like in those days. Can you see the kettle boiling on the hob? Well that was the only source of hot water for most families in those days. These were very small houses with just two bedrooms, no bathroom and a toilet down the yard. There were often six or seven children and some of my friends here had as many as eleven children in their families. Our mums had a very hard job keeping our homes and the family clean. It was a much harder job than it is today, with many more chores to be done such as black-leading the hearth, donkey-stoning the front step, or even whitewashing the backyard. Everything had to be done by hand and so the housework took much longer to do. These small terraced houses had no electricity and many had just one cold water tap. Can you imagine what it must have been like?

We are going to start by showing you some things that were used a lot in our homes and we will tell you what they were called and what they were used for."

Although our performances are now improvised, they do follow a set format. We begin by introducing the first household item – the dolly tub – and go on to demonstrate a typical washday, which, for most families, would be on a Monday. We explain that clothes, including underwear, were only changed once a week, on Saturdays. So, although people had far fewer clothes to wash, they would have been pretty grubby by the end of the week. We demonstrate all the chores which had to be performed to get the clothes clean, and the hard work which was involved. In those days, all household chores were regarded as women's work, men took no part in them. We all remember our mothers' swollen red hands after washday.

Lighting the boiler was the first job, then filling it with the water to be heated. The dolly tub had to be filled with water by hand, before putting in the soda crystals and finally the first batch of dirty clothes. We show how the dolly peg was twisted and turned amongst the dirty washing in order to loosen all the dirt, and the posher pushed up and down, to force all the dirt

Horses and carts, rattling along cobbled streets, were common in the 1930s.

We show the children the type of toys, often homemade from household scraps and leftovers, which children played with in the 1930s.

'Connie Onnie', or condensed milk, was an important part of the 1930s' diet.

out. Badly soiled clothes had to be soaked first to remove some of the dirt, often in the Saturday night bath water! After a good poshing in the dolly tub, they were then rubbed on the washboard, particularly the men's white collars and cuffs, which were then transferred to the boiler to be boiled. White clothes were often washed in water with a bag of 'blue' added to make them look whiter.

After washing, the clothes had to be rinsed thoroughly in fresh water, at least three times, which meant the dolly tub had to be emptied and refilled three times as well. Some things had to be starched, which was an extra chore, and last, but not least, everything had to be passed through the mangle to squeeze out as much water as possible. Wringing out the cumbersome wet clothes was probably the most arduous job of all. Large sheets and blankets, which were particularly heavy and unwieldy when wet, would be twisted and then draped in folds over the woman's arm, to be fed into the mangle. At the end of the day, the poor woman, who might well have been pregnant, or have very young children, or both, would be soaking wet and completely exhausted. Tea that night would usually be Sunday's leftovers fried up.

The next day was usually ironing day. People did not have ironing boards. Instead, they put a folded sheet or blanket on the kitchen table and ironed on that. The flat irons themselves were made of cast iron and most people had two: one to be heating, while the other was being used to iron the clothes. The iron was heated on the fire, or on a gas ring, as there was no electricity in people's homes in those days. A wad of cloth was needed to lift it off the fire because it would get very hot. Housewives would turn the newly-heated iron upside down and spit on it. If the spit sizzled and bounced off the iron quickly, then it was hot enough to use. It then had to be wiped on another cloth to clean away any soot or ash. Because the irons did not produce any steam, each item to be ironed had to first be splashed with water and then rolled up for the water to disperse evenly through the garment, making the creases fall out more easily.

The next item to be shown to the children is the shoe last and again we explain its use to them. We tell them that in the thirties all shoes were made of leather, even the soles, which wore out very quickly. Often, when a small hole first appeared in the sole, a piece of cardboard would be pushed inside the shoe. Only when the hole grew to a certain size, did the shoe merit a new sole. It was a regular thing for children to see their dads mending the family's shoes and boots. First he would buy a big piece of leather from the cobbler and then the shoe would be fitted onto the last. This was a very heavy iron object with three sides, each one shaped like the sole of a shoe. There was a very small one for toddlers' shoes, a medium one for ladies' shoes and a large one for men's shoes. It provided a strong, durable base to hammer on. A piece of leather would be laid onto the bottom of the worn out shoe and tacked into place with a hammer and sprigs, which were special nails for mending shoes. Then the leather was carefully cut into the shape of the sole of the shoe, after which it was filed smooth and something called 'Heelball', which looked like black wax, was melted over a candle flame and smoothed around the edge of the shoe. Any leather left over was not wasted, but was used for heel or toe tips – not a scrap was wasted.

We go on to explain that some people could not afford leather and would use the rubber from an old tyre to repair their shoes and that shoes were always worn and worn until they were completely beyond repair. When a child grew out of his or her shoes, or clothes, they were never thrown away, instead they were handed down to someone smaller than they were, usually a younger brother or sister.

At this point the narrator returns and comments on the drudgery entailed in washing and ironing in the thirties.

"It took two whole days to do the family wash. Not a bit like today where everything goes into the washing machine and the whole procedure is done in little more than an hour. Lots of today's clothing is designed to need little or no ironing. Our mums had no washing machines, or vacuum cleaners either. We didn't even have carpets. Our floors were scrubbed with carbolic soap and a scrubbing brush – no wonder their skin was always red and raw and their hands painful and misshapen with rheumatism.

Then there was shopping, so very different then than it is today …"

We ask the children if any of them have recently been to the supermarket with their mums and dads and what it was like – the automatic door opening as you walk in with the trolley, then filling it up from the shelves displaying a massive assortment of elaborately-packaged goods. The lady at the checkout runs it all over a panel and the cost of the goods comes up on the screen. The automatic till even tells you how much change you will get.

"Our shopping was not a bit like that," says the narrator. "Would you like to see how it was done? Well, come over to our corner shop and we'll show you."

Three customers come to the shop for various items and one child is selected to run an errand, carrying a note. The first customer asks for a donkey stone, to clean the front step, a gas mantle, used on the gas pipe to distribute the light, and some candles. She also asks for two ounces of cheese for her husband's 'carry out' (packed lunch). This customer also asks for 'tick', or credit, as she has no more money until her husband's next pay day.

The second customer is carrying a cup and she asks the shopkeeper for a cup of jam. She also asks for two slices of bacon and four ounces of margarine. It is pointed out to the children that ordinary people had very little money to spare, so they bought food in very small quantities and also, with no fridge, had nowhere to store perishable food. The same customer also asks for two ounces of tea and a bottle of 'Aunt Sally' (disinfectant).

Then a volunteer child enters with the note. He has been sent to buy a bundle of chips (firewood) and a tin of 'Connie Onnie' (condensed milk). The third customer wants two cracked eggs, which were then used to make custard, or a cake and, of course, they were cheaper than unbroken ones. Almost nothing was wasted in those days. She also asks for two pennyworth of broken biscuits, a loaf and two ounces of brawn (a preparation of meat made from pig's head and ox feet, cut up, boiled and pickled) which, when mashed with potatoes, made a light and inexpensive meal. Finally, Mrs Roberts dashes in at the last minute for a bar of carbolic soap. It's bath night!

Barbara helps a child volunteer to weigh out small quantities of dry goods. Housewives usually shopped daily and bought food in very small quantities.

Ovaltine, though still available today, somehow conjures up an image of the 1930s and 40s.

Bath night used to be quite a performance in the 1930s and the entire ritual is re-enacted in our workshop using children as volunteers.

To keep the scenes fresh, roles are regularly exchanged in the workshops, including the role of narrator.

The narrator now returns and moves the children back to the house scene. It is Saturday night – bath night.

She asks the audience to raise their hands if they have had a bath or shower in the last day or two. All the children raise their hands at once, but the teachers often just sit there. The narrator says to the children in an aside: "Miss (or Sir) has not had a bath or shower!" This always goes down well with the children and the teachers hurriedly raise their hands.

"Now what was your bath night like?" she asks. "You turned on the tap and nice hot water came out. In went the bubble bath, followed by you. You played for a bit, then mum washed your hair, got you out and dried you with a nice fluffy towel. Then you went downstairs and Mum dried your hair with the hairdryer. Was it something like that?"

The children invariably all agree.

"Well, it wasn't like that in our day. Shall we show you what it was like?" she asks.

The bath night scene is set in a small house. This time 'grandmother' explains what is about to happen. She calls eight children up from the audience to illustrate how cramped an area they lived in. Most homes housed large families. 'Mother', or 'Mrs Roberts' then comes in carrying a bucket of cold water, a scrubbing brush and a bar of strong-smelling carbolic soap. She is also carrying the baby in her other arm. She listens as her mother tells her children off for playing out so late. Mrs Roberts then hands her baby to one of the children, usually a boy, to hold, and tells him not to make her cry. This again causes some laughter from the children. At this stage we ask for two volunteers, a boy and a girl, to demonstrate the bath night procedure. We have the children take up the rag rug in front of the fire and lay down papers to soak up any spilled water. Two other children are sent to fetch the bath from the wall in the backyard and are warned not to scream if there are any spiders in it.

Mother now pretends to fill the bath with tepid water to prevent scalds, testing it with her elbow, and then commences to bath the girl. She washes her hair with carbolic soap and jokes with gran about her dirty neck and the cabbages growing behind her ears. She threatens to scrub her knees and elbows with the scrubbing brush and also mentions the dirt between her toes. The girl then gets out of the bath with a towel round her. Gran takes over at this point, and while she is drying her and putting her nightie on, mother reminds her to check her hair for nits.

The boy then kneels by the bath to have his hair washed. As he does so, mother hears his chest wheezing. "Oh! Tommy," she says, "your chest sounds bad, I'll have to give it a good rub with some camphorated oil." She puts on his combinations and proceeds to rub his chest with the oil and while she does so, the group sings, *Our Poor Tommy has a Cold upon his Chest*. The children are then sent up to bed carrying the potty and some strips of newspaper, instead of toilet paper. Other children are asked to tidy up and put the rag rug back in place in front of the fire. Mother and gran then sit down for a nice cup of tea.

The narrator returns to ask the children what they thought about our bath night. Often they say it would have been fun. But she says, "Well, I don't think your mums would have liked it." She reminds them that eight children have been bathed in the one bathful of water, with just an extra drop of hot water added to keep it warm. "It must have been like pea soup when the last child got in," she says.

The narrator then moves on to talk to the children about a very important subject in a child's life: playtime and toys. She reminds the children that many families in Liverpool during the 1930s had very little money to live on and could not afford to buy their children any toys. The best they could do was to make them, or clean up and paint old secondhand toys. We have a selection of homemade toys like the ones we played with as children. Dolls made of old socks, or knitted, with buttons for eyes. We show the children how these are made. We have tin cans threaded with twine to walk on and stilts, bats and balls, whizzers made with coat buttons, and kites. There are cigarette cards, yo-yos and jacks and ollies (marbles). We tell the children about the street games we used to play, and how our mums would turn the rope for us while we all skipped together, and the skipping songs that we sang. Some time is spent letting the children try out these toys, and some of us have a skip with them.

We ask if the children would like to sing some of their playtime songs. Some need a little coaxing, but others are more willing. There are a few minutes more for questions that the children might like to ask about our childhood, and then the session ends with another song, this time with actions – *Underneath the Spreading Chestnut Tree*.

Margaret holds up a pair of longjohns on bath night – the children find them highly amusing.

1940s Workshop

As the 1930s came to an end, people were very much aware that there was going to be a war. The fact that there would be a shortage of some foods and commodities presented no particular hardship for working class families. Poverty, caused by mass unemployment, already meant us going without many things. We were not, however, prepared for all the other horror and sadness that war brings, both physical and emotional.

We start this workshop by welcoming the children in our usual way, making an archway with our arms and singing them in with an appropriate song. Vera's husband, Pat, accompanies us on his mouth organ. This makes a light-hearted and fun start to what is after all, a history lesson, one which we know they will enjoy, by what they write in their letters to us.

Once the children are settled, the narrator explains to them that in the following scenes, the group will try to show them what being at war, and living through those times, was really like. She will explain to them that this is our story, we are telling them about our own personal memories of these times. She begins by introducing three members of the group, each of whom will show the children artefacts which were familiar to everyone during the war, and in each case a child will be asked to help demonstrate its use.

The first items are the gas masks; there were three types. The standard one was issued to children of seven and over, and also to adults. The second, a coloured one with a funny-shaped nose, was called the Mickey Mouse gas mask, and this one was for the very young children. The third was a large one, for babies. The baby had to be put into the mask headfirst, with just its legs exposed and it was tied securely with tapes around the baby's waist. There was a small hand pump at the side which the mother worked to give the baby air. We use a doll to demonstrate to the children what it must have been like for a mother to put her baby into such a contraption. For although we never had need to use the gas masks, we still had to be prepared and to practise putting them on quickly from time to time. Also, the mother would probably have other very young children to attend to as well as herself and the baby – supposing she had twins! The gas masks were carried around in a box on a piece of string. Young women used to sew or crochet covers for the masks to match their outfits.

The next item is a stirrup pump. This is a hand-operated pump with a hose attached and a footrest shaped like a stirrup, hence the name. The main function of the pump was to put out fires caused by incendiary bombs, which the enemy dropped in order to light up their targets. We explain, of course, how dark it was in the blackout, with not the tiniest glimmer of light showing anywhere. We tell them how every street had a number of these pumps, along with buckets of water and sand. When an incendiary bomb was dropped, speed was of the utmost importance. We have two children to help

The scene of devastation after an air-raid was truly shocking.

Molly shows the children a jagged piece of shrapnel and explains what it is.

Margaret and Nina listening to a recording of Chamberlain's declaration of war on the radio.

with this, one to work the pump and the other to hose the water onto the bombs. We also have a real incendiary bomb, lent to us by the museum, to show them.

Shrapnel is next; named after William Shrapnel, who invented the bomb of that name. Shrapnel is the metal outer casing of exploded bombs, and the shells from the ack-ack (anti-aircraft) guns. After an air-raid, jagged pieces of shrapnel were scattered all over the city streets. The boys would run out from the shelters and collect it, all trying to find the best piece. It was a highly-prized collector's item amongst the lads. It was also lethal; many people were killed after being struck by it during the raids. And many of the children who collected it cut their hands, it was so sharp.

After the artefacts have been demonstrated, the narrator returns and says a few words about the changes that were going on around us; Anderson air-raid shelters were being issued and built in backyards and large, communal brick shelters in the streets. For the elderly, and those with mobility problems, as well as those who did not have a backyard or access to a brick shelter, very large, reinforced metal 'tables' were issued. During an air raid people would crawl underneath the table and be reasonably well protected from falling masonry etc. We had all been given gas masks, and sandbags were being packed around all the important buildings in town. Windows were criss-crossed with tape to stop flying glass and fitted with blackout curtains to stop any light from escaping.

The narrator explains that the blackout was designed to prevent enemy bombers from finding their targets. She tells the children how all vehicles, including bicycles, had to have their headlamps painted green, or covered in gauze, leaving only a narrow slit of light in the middle. To help people find their way in the dark, kerbstones were painted white and a white circle was painted around lampposts.

The narrator then takes us back to the day that war commenced. The scene opens with two sisters waiting anxiously by the wireless in a house in Liverpool. The Prime Minister is about to address the nation. A recording of Neville Chamberlain's speech is played and the women are very distressed when they hear him declare that we are now at war with Germany. Their worst fears have now become a reality; not only will their husbands and older sons be called up, but also their children will have to be evacuated. They have no idea where they will be going, or who they will be staying with.

A boy and girl from the audience volunteer to be evacuees, and they help to pack their clothes into a pillowslip. One of the mothers explains that we had no suitcases, because we never needed them, as no one could afford holidays. Each child has just one change of clothes, no slippers or dressing gown, no toothpaste either, we were told to use salt. The boy is shown a pair of combinations, an all-in-one undersuit, and is told that his grandad has kindly given them to him to wear so that he will be warm and the girl is given a long flannelette nightie belonging to her mother. These two items, not forgetting the boy's short trousers, create a great deal of laughter. The mothers keep urging the children to stay together, and to send home the postcards they have been given, as soon as possible, with their new address on, "so your mam will know where you are". They tell their children not to let them down, to keep themselves tidy and clean and not to go anywhere without their gas masks.

The narrator returns and asks the children if they are good at pretending, because they are now all going to be evacuees, going on a long journey to some unknown place. The children move to the scene of a reception centre in a small Welsh village. The billeting officer welcomes them, and introduces them to the district nurse, who lines them up to inspect their teeth and nails and asks them to put out their tongues so that she can tell if they need to be given worm cake. This always causes a lot of laughter, because we include the teachers in this exercise too.

Local residents now come to the centre to take some children home with them, depending on how large their homes are. A Welsh lady arrives with her daughter Blodwen. They live in a tiny cottage, so Blodwen will choose just one little girl who will share her bedroom. Lots of the girls want to go with Blodwen, and her mum is so sorry that she cannot take any more children into her home.

A farmer's wife comes in next; she wants six strong boys who can help on the farm, to take the place of the farm hands who have joined the Army. There are lots of volunteers, and six boys are chosen. The farmer's wife feels their muscles. She tells them how hard the work is, feeding the pigs and mucking out the cowsheds, as well as helping with the harvest. The boys are usually quite happy about the work, until they learn that they have to go to school as well!

Lady Maude is the next to appear with her little doggie Fifi resting in her shopping basket. She is the typical lady of the manor and always makes the adults smile. Dressed to the nines with a double fox fur draped around her shoulders, and wearing a little black hat with a veil, she is an out and out snob! She bemoans the fact that her butler and all the gardeners have been called up and her maids have gone off to work on munitions, so she has been left horribly short-staffed. Lady Maude now needs six girls to come and stay with her. She tells the six girls she chooses what their duties will be, housework, gardening, looking after the puppies, and, of course, making Lady Maude's tea!

The narrator returns to the scene. Time has moved on. She tells the children how at that time the war was raging at sea, with the German U boats attacking our ships to prevent vital supplies from reaching the country. Thousands of our men were losing their lives at sea. At home it was quiet. In many ways things seemed no different from how they had been before. Because the threat of German bombers seemed to have receded, many children returned home from the evacuation after only a few months. A great many of them were very homesick and their mums missed them too. Also, not all the children were looked after properly, though some were more fortunate than others.

Not long after they came home, the bombing did begin. The enemy planes arrived with a vengeance. People began to realise just why all the elaborate precautions had been taken, such as the blackout, the air-raid shelters, the sandbags placed around the buildings, and the emergency water supplies at the end of most streets.

Preparing for evacuation – packing a few essential belongings into a pillowcase.

Upon arrival, the evacuees were allocated a foster family. Here 'Lady Maude' selects suitable evacuees to replace her maids and gardeners who have all left to do war work.

The narrator now takes the children back to Liverpool.

The next scene is inside a house, where a woman is preparing to go to the air-raid shelter for the night. She is putting sandwiches, water, candles and a blanket into a box to take with her. She demonstrates a simple device which was used at the time – two flower pots, one on top of the other, with a candle inside – which gave a dim light and could double up as a hand-warmer in the cold, damp shelter. She also shows another popular idea which was used in the shelters; a scarf was partly sewn up down one side to made a hood and muffler in one, ideal to keep warm in the shelter. Such simple, homely devices were very typical of the make-do-and-mend mentality which was encouraged at the time.

The woman is worried about her sister Annie, who went out hours ago with the ration books to try and get some food. Suddenly Annie comes running in with news about the destruction everywhere, and how the shops have been bombed and people having to walk miles to find anywhere open. The authorities had had to send for more sand from Formby to meet the demand for more sandbags. She also speaks of the awful tragedies she has heard about – friends and neighbours killed, horses lying dead in the street and buildings smouldering in ruins.

Two children volunteer to carry the box to the shelter, along with the potty and the *Liverpool Echo* cut into squares and threaded on string. Annie grumbles that she has not read it yet, as they move off to the shelter. The air-raid siren wails its warning. Annie has to run back to the house for the insurance policies and the ration books. Then the bombing starts (we have a tape-recorded air-raid) and all the lights are dimmed. The air-raid warden (Vera's husband, Pat) shouts, "Put that light out!" The children duck under their seats until the 'all clear' sounds. This scene obviously has the greatest impact on the children, because it is mentioned in the majority of their letters.

The lights are turned on again and the narrator returns to the scene. She says how terrifying the raid had been. She then asks the children to say what they think it would be like after a really bad air-raid. They speak of the damaged buildings, people who have been hurt and killed, great holes made by the bombs etc. Many of them think that the streets would probably be empty and we tell them what it was actually like. The narrator says, "we will go back to the house now, after this long air-raid and see what happens next."

A grandmother is trying to clear up her home after the raid. It is full of dust from the blast of the bombs and part of her ceiling has collapsed. Two of the children (pretending to be her grandchildren) are helping her. Their home has been destroyed in the raid and their mother has gone out to look for water. The grandmother explains that there is no gas or electricity, and no water in any of the homes.

Another daughter arrives with one of her children and the baby. There is an unexploded bomb in their street and they have had to leave their home

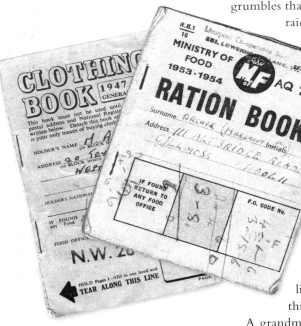

Barbara with a young volunteer in a scene depicting what it was like after an air-raid.

Ration books and insurance policies were always taken into the shelter during an air-raid.

until it is made safe for them to return. She is upset at hearing the news about her sister being bombed out and losing everything she had.

They hear the sound of voices and Doris returns with some children who have helped her to carry the buckets of water. She says that she has had to go quite a long way to find it, and had to queue in a long line of people. She has spilled some carrying it back over the piles of rubble in the streets. She tells of the devastation everywhere, of buildings still ablaze and anxious people walking around, frantically trying to find relatives who lived in the area. She tells her mother about a neighbour's five little boys who have been killed sheltering in the cellar, where their mother thought they would be safe. Doris, already very upset at the loss of her own home, starts to cry. (There is not a dry eye in the house. This scene always touches everyone, us as well). Mother and sister try to comfort Doris, they pour out some tea and start making plans to go to the food office the next day about the loss of her ration books and wondering where she should go about the loss of her home. It is pointed out to the children that these were some of the many the problems that a lot of women had to deal with on their own.

The siren sounds again. The children dive under their chairs once more, but this time the warden cries, "False alarm!" We point out that we did have many of these, too.

The narrator brings the session to a close by telling the children that in spite of the dreadful bombing and all the sadness of war, people still tried to make the best of things:

"We carried on with our lives as usual; going to the pictures and dances, having parties, though there were no delicious buffets laid on like we have today. Entertainment was very important to us; it kept up our morale. We sang in the air-raid shelters to entertain ourselves, but mainly it helped to drown out the sound of the bombing outside."

We conclude the performance by singing a typical wartime song, encouraging the children to join in. *The Quartermaster's Store* is a favourite. Often the children offer to sing their own version of this song and other wartime songs too. We also allow some time at the end of the session for questions which the children might like to ask us. We wave goodbye to them with another wartime song, *Wish Me Luck As You Wave Me Goodbye*.

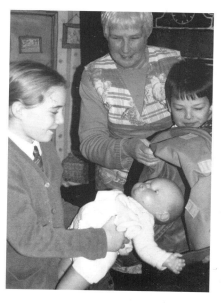

We, as a group, never cease to be amazed by the enthusiasm of the children during our sessions at the museum. There is never a shortage of volunteers, some children would be in every scene given the chance. We do however try to ensure that most them are given the chance to take part, by leaving it to the teacher to choose. Their questions leave us in no doubt that we have had their full attention throughout the scenes, and that they have understood what we were presenting.

The reader may ask how we acquired all the information to impart to the children. The simple answer is — we lived it. The following pages are our stories. Where and how we lived, and how we worked and played.

Vera shows the children a real incendiary bomb and describes what it was used for.

Barbara demonstrates the cumbersome, large, gas mask which was used for babies. Once the baby was inside, the mask had to be pumped to maintain an air supply.

The actual incendiary bomb used in the workshop.

Phyl Kenny – Born 1916

I was born in Birmingham in 1916 in the middle of the First World War. I made my first appearance at eleven o'clock on a Sunday morning, so my birth stopped my mother from going to church. She was a regular churchgoer and did a lot for our local church. She washed and starched the choir's surplices, went to mothers' meetings and sent her children to a church school.

Yes on that Sunday morning a star fell from heaven – flat on my face, for I am no oil painting! A relative once unkindly asked me if I had caught my nose in a bottle – but I did not care. I have heard it said that a long nose denotes strength of character.

To return to that fateful day. My father took one look at me and exclaimed, "Another bobtailed one!" He already had a five-year-old daughter and was hoping for a son. Disappointed, he decided there and then to answer Earl Haig's call to join the forces and fight for King and Country and mum was left to bring up two children on her own. I often heard my mum say how hard life was at that time. To satisfy her gnawing hunger before going to bed, she would often eat a piece of bread and lard.

Before long my mother received the devastating news that dad had been reported missing, presumed dead. But he was still alive. He was a prisoner of war. He had been shot in the arm and then found by a German soldier who treated him kindly, putting a cigarette in his mouth. When he finally came home, dad would never speak ill of the ordinary German soldier, he said they were just like us; short of rations and only wanting to go home to their wives and children. I don't remember his homecoming, I suppose I was too young.

We lived in a small two-up-two-down house in a secluded close with a small garden that was dad's pride and joy. The toilets were down the yard and had to be shared with four other families. I clearly remember one morning near my fifth birthday, when I was skipping along the backyard on the way back from the toilet, swinging my potty backwards and forwards. I met a neighbour and proudly told her, "I've got a new baby brother". Dad had his wish come true.

I started primary school at about the same time. Schools were very cold places in those days and if you worked hard at lessons and did well, you were

Many women from poor families took in washing to supplement their meagre incomes. Phyl's mother washed anything and everything, from church surplices to butchers' aprons, to secure a better life for her family.

allowed to get warm by the coke fire at the end of the room. The teachers were very strict and if you misbehaved you were sent to the headmistress, who would hit you on the hand with the cane. On one occasion I was given one lash for giggling in class. I didn't dare tell my mother who, if she had found out, would only have said that I deserved it. The education we received was very sound, but quite limited, and didn't go far enough as regards maths or literature.

Sewing and knitting were felt to be important skills for a girl to learn and I picked up the art of knitting from my mum. During the war years I knitted many pairs of gloves on two knitting needles.

At eleven I sat and failed the grammar school exam, but at fourteen I gained a place at a commercial college, which I reluctantly declined to accept, deciding instead to take a job as an office clerk to help with family finances. Dad was only working two or three days a week and my older sister was already working in a clerk's job at a bicycle manufacturers. Wages were very low for everybody – the recession was beginning to bite.

Illness of one kind or another was very common in those days and, at about this time, our family's health seemed to deteriorate for some reason. My sister developed St Vitus' Dance (Chorea), a nervous disease causing irregular, involuntary movements of the limbs and face, and I had a painful bout of shingles. Most worrying of all, my brother was diagnosed with meningitis, which made him seriously ill, and he was in hospital for many months. Every Sunday in church, the congregation would be asked to pray for 'little Jimmy Smith'.

As we struggled to recover from this bad patch, Mum decided she wanted a better life for her family and was determined to do something about it. The family income was soon being supplemented by the taking in of even more washing – in addition to the church surplices, she washed anything and everything, including workmen's and butchers' overalls. On wet days the house was full of steam and dripping clothes. There was also the ironing to be done, which took her hours. Like most children, I hated to be singled out and felt ashamed if I met any of my friends when pushing the old pram full of clean clothes back to their owners. Mum then became a housekeeper in a huge mansion of a house, which, at one time, had actually been attached to the house next door. We lived in the servants' quarters. The cellars were enormous and were used to store food and wine, there being no refrigerators at that time. I particularly remember eggs pickled in isinglass (a material, mainly gelatine, got from sturgeons' air bladders and other sources) and stored down there until they were needed.

Dad continued with his three days a week job and also tended the garden. There was always a good smell of cooking in the house and we took homemade rock cakes to the office for our colleagues. Sometimes, outside the office, a man with a hurdy-gurdy and a monkey would play the latest tunes and wait for us to throw coppers to him. It made our day.

My first introduction to Liverpool was in 1939. I came with my then future husband to meet his parents and I remember it well because it was snowing heavily as we arrived. Oh! Didn't it snow! I had never seen so much snow. It was still snowing when we took the late train back to Birmingham.

At the best of times the journey took about three and a half-hours. The engine pulled a number of carriages in which a series of compartments were connected by a corridor, running along one side, which led to the toilets. There were no refreshment facilities. We were very tired, having spent a hectic few days meeting his family and friends, and we both fell asleep. When I awoke the train was not moving and there was no sound of any kind; no movement outside or in. At first I thought everyone was dead and that I was the sole survivor. Gingerly I crept along the corridor, looking into each compartment, but all was well. Everybody seemed to be sleeping and outside everything was white. I still could not tell where we were. It was a very weird experience. We eventually moved off and arrived safely at New Street Station.

I was quite a shy person before I came to Liverpool, and only wanted a very quiet wedding, preferably mid-week, when everyone was working, and at the Registry Office. For one thing, we six made a strange group. The groom had lost an eye in an accident at work. I had been suffering severe toothache for a fortnight and had been forcibly taken to a dentist for the removal of all my top teeth. My mother-in-law had lost an eye as a child, and my father-in-law had been severely burned about the face and arms in France during World War 1 and had no ears. My mother, well! She was the belle of the ball and she stole the show. The best man was a cousin and he, too, looked good in his RAF uniform. His company was stationed not far away. So that was the wedding picture. Two guests, each with one eye, one with no ears and me with no top teeth! Is there any wonder I wanted only a quiet wedding?

Liverpool was the chosen venue for our honeymoon. We spent it cycling to Freshfield and Southport and on a trip on the ferry to New Brighton. We thoroughly enjoyed it.

It was near the end of 1940 when we decided to relocate to Liverpool. The war had started and we had been subjected to heavy air-raids in Birmingham. We had spent as much as thirteen hours outside in the Anderson shelter some nights. Bombs had been dropped all around the area. Our front door had been blown off, windows shattered and there was soot all over my mum's new rug. It was absolutely terrifying. Each evening saw a general exodus of families pushing prams laden with their most treasured belongings, to find safer places in shelters, in the parks, or wherever. I was pregnant, so my kind in-laws persuaded us to come and stay with them, because Liverpool seemed comparatively safe at the time. How wrong we were. Hitler's bombers swiftly followed us to Liverpool.

We now lived in Walton and my baby was to be delivered in Walton Hospital. In the not too distant past the hospital had been a workhouse and was still a forbidding, dismal building. Due to the wartime activities, mothers and their babies only stayed one night after delivery and, provided there were no complications, were then evacuated to a mansion in Southport which once had belonged to a disgraced financier, who was in jail.

When my contractions began, I was admitted, naive and scared, to the labour ward. I felt that the nursing staff were unfeeling and brusque in their treatment of patients and made no allowances for the fact that this was my

Remember When ...

Birth and Childhood

- When newborn babies were taken out for an airing they wore a veil over their face.

- It was considered good luck for visitors to put a piece of silver in the new baby's hand.

- New mothers were confined to bed for two weeks and not fed ordinary food, but gruel, which was a thin porridge, made with milk.

- It was thought to bring bad luck if the new mother visited before being churched (attending a special church service).

- Newborn babies wore long clothes for six weeks after their birth. It was an occasion when the baby was 'shortened' (put into short clothes), usually on a Sunday.

- Boys wore dresses until they were nearly five years of age, and were not given a boy's haircut until then.

Phyl was relieved to get her new baby home from the regimented routine of Walton Hospital, where the nurses were brusque and the building, once an old workhouse, was dismal and depressing.

first baby. They were kept very busy running to and fro between the labour and delivery wards and it did not help my confidence to hear the screams and moans coming from other poor souls about to give birth.

In the delivery room we were handed a mask and told to breathe deeply if the pain became too much (I think it was supposed to contain ether). Although I had an urgent desire to push, I was made to wait until a midwife was available, it being the rule that a midwife must be in attendance at the birth. I needed several stitches after the birth and only after the doctor had completed the stitching did he discover that my mask had no gas in it. No wonder I was doing a bit of yelling!

Patients were only allowed visitors twice a week – on Wednesdays and Sundays – and then only two to each bed. The hospital was run on very regimented lines, not like the relaxed atmosphere which prevails today. I prayed to be moved to Southport, as rumour had it that the mansion was like heaven compared to the depressing conditions at the hospital, but complications, in the form of thrombosis, prevented me from going. The patient in the next bed (and the beds were crammed very close together) had to be treated for head lice, and my bedside cabinet was swarming with ants. I was thoroughly miserable.

This situation was endured for three weeks, after which I was taken back to my family with my little 'bundle of love', only to experience the May Blitz. During one raid – a false alarm – I grabbed the baby in his basket and dived under the table to find a bottle of whisky planted there. Grabbing the bottle and taking a generous swig, I thought, "well at least we can die happy".

We soon found a house to rent and tried to settle down to married life. One evening, after I had bathed and fed the baby and laid him down to sleep, I happened to look in the direction of the bath towels hanging on the clothes airer to dry, and to my horror, saw four large cockroaches crawling all over them. It soon became abundantly clear that they were not the only ones; the house was alive with them. Over the next few years I must have killed thousands of the filthy pests, but they just kept on multiplying. They came in all shapes and sizes. When we first discovered them, we emptied the room, tore out the skirting boards, and put 'Steam-fly' and various other powders down to kill, or at least deter them. I also used to creep downstairs at night, switch on the light and rush around stamping on them, or battering them before they could scurry away. Next morning I would shovel up the disgusting brown corpses and put fresh powder down. I began to wonder if they were invading our home, or we theirs, or if the powder was actually attracting them from my neighbours' houses.

Food rationing was also a big problem. If, while out shopping, I happened to see a group of women outside a shop, I would join them in the hope that they were queueing for something edible. On one occasion it was for half a rabbit and the shopkeeper came out, surveyed the queue, saw me and shouted, "And you need not stay! You're not a customer of mine". So no rabbit pie that day. However, there was a general feeling of goodwill and helpfulness among neighbours, who soon passed on the word when fresh deliveries were spotted going into shops. Fruit was almost non-existent and the Government encouraged us to grow our own vegetables – mostly carrots and potatoes. I took my baby to the local clinic for orange juice and cod liver oil and the radio doctor every morning gave us advice on health and diet, but we did not like Lord Road's National Wheatmeal Loaf, nor whale meat, which was introduced into the diet by John Strachey, who was minister for food. He was concerned about the low fat and meat content of the nation's diet. Whale meat had the consistency of meat, but was rather chewy and oily and tasted fishy. It was just about acceptable if nothing else was available. The Groundnuts (peanuts) scheme was started in Africa to provide us with vegetable oil, but it was a complete fiasco. The wrong kind of soil coupled with a drought, completely ruined a whole year's crop.

Phyl in 1948, aged thirty-two, with her two sons, aged five and seven.

During the coal crisis we burned anything and everything to keep the fire going in the winter and it was a struggle to keep warm. But all was not gloom and doom. The cinemas, theatres and ballrooms still operated for those willing to take a chance on there being an air-raid that night. Radio producers did their best to create a sense of normality by playing music and putting on programmes like *Workers' Playtime, ITMA, The Brain's Trust* and many others.

I am one of the survivors of the war, but I would not wish to live through an experience like that again, and I think all war is barbaric. My husband was a very kind, caring man and a wonderful father. He had seen what the First World War had done to his father, and my father, and to many others. He was very politically-minded and did not think the Government had done enough to avoid going to war. He had also read that we were still trading with Germany after the First World War had been declared and so refused, when he was called up, to have any part in it and became a conscientious objector.

Consequently he was hauled before a tribunal of old men every six months, to restate his conscientious objections, conditional upon his staying in the job he then had (a milkman), and was not allowed to earn more than thirty shillings a week. Having two young children and a wife to support meant that life was extremely bleak. Also we had ill-informed neighbours putting notes through the letterbox implying that he was a coward, which he most certainly was not, as anyone who went through these tribunals could confirm. He was also the first out of doors putting out fires caused by the incendiary bombs that were dropping everywhere. His young brother, who was barely eighteen years old, and had never been away from home, was sent to Walton and then Staffordshire jails among hardened criminals for holding the same views regarding the war.

Doris Windsor – Born 1917

I was born in October 1917, in Seaforth, the second child in the family; my brother Norman was a year and nine months older than me. Mother was left at home with two small babies, very upset that my dad had volunteered for the Army. She could not understand his motives; he was not a fighter, or adventurous in any way. He was a quiet man, who never drank or smoked, it was quite out of character. I strongly suspect that he was more afraid of being dubbed a coward, than he was of joining up. He was the youngest of a family of six, spoiled and loved greatly. His eldest brother Dick was killed at the battle of the Somme, his other brother Bob, was taken prisoner in France, and his sister Margaret died within six weeks of Dick's death. His other brother was not medically fit, so I think dad felt compelled to join up. He was away for almost three years, coming home in 1919.

We lived in a two-up-two-down terraced house with no hot water, and a toilet in the yard. Mother used to tell us of how she trudged with two babies in the pram from Seaforth to Great Homer Street, just to obtain some food. Another baby, a son, was born in 1919, and they went on to have eleven children in all: seven boys and four girls. Life was an uphill struggle.

When dad was demobbed in 1919, he was profoundly deaf and unable to get a decent job because of his impairment. His deafness was due to the damp conditions in Army camps which had caused a chronic middle ear infection. Although an intelligent man, his deafness made him withdrawn and unable to mix. He eventually obtained a hearing aid when the Labour Party brought in the National Health Scheme in 1948. His whole life consisted of reading the *Liverpool Echo*, solving crossword puzzles, and making 'Bullets' which was a competition in the *John Bull* magazine. He had little money to enter competitions himself, so he handed over his efforts to friends, who sent them in, and did manage to win small prizes.

I remember sitting round the scrubbed table covered with oilcloth, which was easy to wipe clean. The corners were always rough and patchy, where the top layer had pealed off. Mother sat at one end, deftly cutting bread with the current baby on her knee, dad in his chair, the only one with arms, reading aloud a murder case in the *Echo*. He had a resonant voice, a good reader, and we as kids were enthralled with the Wallace murder case, and in fact, any

Lewis's as it looked before it was bombed by the Germans in the May Blitz of 1941. It caught fire and went up like a huge furnace.

murder, the grislier the better. I always remember Sir Bernard Spilsbury being mentioned. It seemed to me that a person was hanged on his evidence alone, and I was always very upset when people were hanged, guilty or not. Mrs Van Der Elst used to be outside the prison protesting and although I was only a child, I wanted to carry a banner alongside her.

Saturday night was bath night, and it was always a nightmare. Because there were no fridges in those days, and we had very little money, mother, like lots of other housewives, went shopping on a Saturday night, when the food was sold off more cheaply, rather than it be kept in the shops over the weekend to go bad. As a consequence, I was left in the house with six children to bath, whose ages ranged from three weeks to ten years, when I was a tiny twelve-year-old.

Doris aged twelve (middle), with her two sisters, Phyllis and Muriel.

I had to fill the boiler from the kitchen tap and light a fire under it using paper, wood chips and coal. In order to keep the water warm enough for the children to be bathed, I had to supplement the hot water from the boiler with kettles and pans of hot water, which I heated on the hob in the other room. The next job was to drag the heavy zinc bath in from its nail in the yard. The bath then had to be filled with the hot water from the boiler, which entailed putting in cold water first, then topping it up with hot. I had to make sure the children were bathed in order, with the youngest child being first, so he could be put to bed first.

On one particular night, all was going well until the baby started crying, and I had to attend to him. My brother, Ivor, the next eldest, at ten years old, asked if he could help. As the water in the kettle had mostly been used up, I asked him to refill it. He removed the lid from the hot kettle before he reached the tap and the escaping steam burned his hand. With a yelp of pain, he dropped the kettle. The boiling water that it still contained spilled down his bare legs and feet, badly scalding him, and he cried out even more loudly. The other children started to scream as well. I was terrified that my mother was going to blame me. I was still in charge of the other children and I didn't know what to do. All I could think of was to send for an adult to help and I sent the next eldest child, Phyllis, aged about eight, to fetch a neighbour, but they were all out shopping for cheap food as well. In desperation, I emptied the flour bag on the burn, because I thought this was clean and dry.

I can still hear his agonising screams and he bears the scars to this day. I still feel guilty, even though, rationally, I know that I was too young to have been given the responsibility of looking after so many other children, when I was still a child myself. When the doctor eventually came (it was three shillings and sixpence for a visit) he was more concerned about me, and assured me that the leg would eventually heal. My poor mother and dad were so upset about the incident and did not blame me for it in any way. They were not in a pub enjoying themselves; neither of them drank or smoked. It was just the way things were – life was very hard. Society was to blame for allowing this situation to exist and I feel very bitter that folk had to live like that.

Contrary to the majority of people, our washday was on a Tuesday. When we came home from school on a Monday, mother was usually at the old sewing machine in quite a tranquil mood. She would be turning sheets side-to-middle; making someone's old coat into a skirt, trousers, or even a smaller coat; turning up, or letting down hems; darning or sewing on buttons – all in a great effort to keep us all tidy. Not that I appreciated it when she tried Mrs Goodall's old dress on me and decided that, with a hem on it, it would 'do me a turn'. As I was small and very slim, the waistline used to be by my hips, the shoulders halfway down my arms and the washed out grey colour did nothing to flatter my sallow complexion. And the stockings! Grey silk, plaited lisle, which had been on fat legs and had gone out of shape and were far too long. I had to wear these! My short, thin legs would not hold them up, so I got pieces of elastic and tied them as tightly as I possibly could, to try to make these monstrosities look halfway decent. I could do nothing with the width of them, which remained the shape of the previous occupant's fat legs: Norah Batty of the 1930s! No wonder I now have serious varicose veins.

Women who owned a sewing machine could alter and make clothes to fit different members of the family, turn sheets side-to-middle and generally make do and mend. With so many children to clothe, Doris's mother treasured her sewing machine, but Doris did not appreciate all the 'hand-me-downs' which came her way.

On Sundays we always had a lovely dinner: roast potatoes, carrots and turnip and meat. We even had rice pudding to follow. Tea was usually rhubarb and custard, or pineapple chunks, four pence halfpenny a tin. We went to church three times every Sunday. Caradoc Mission morning service and Sunday School, then Evening Service at the Congregational Church in Gladstone Road. I remember some of the speakers at Morning Service. Miss Harding used to remind us 'sinners' of the fires of hell. She always looked at me with her ice blue eyes peering through rimless spectacles. She terrified me. Then there was Miss Johnson, who had been to 'darkest' Africa, where she had brought the story of Jesus to the little pagan black children. We sat wide-eyed as she told us about how the people had leprosy, and their fingers and toes dropped off. Then she persuaded us to take home missionary boxes to collect money for these sick people. We took one home, but I'm sure no money was collected – there was none to spare.

Sundays were very quiet days, no shops or cinemas open. You were not allowed to play noisy games, cut your nails, or sew on the Sabbath. Your best clothes were worn on that day only. People visited relatives or hospitals and then listened to the Palm Court Orchestra on the wireless. My mother used to go to a neighbour's house to play cards, but dad used to ask us to sing all the hymns we had sung in church, so we had another 'church service' before we took off our best clothes, said our prayers and went to bed.

Each summer there was the Sunday School treat. Caradoc Mission took us on the train to the botanical gardens at Churchtown. It was wonderful. There was a monkey house, a palm house, an aviary and a boating lake. It cost sixpence to get a boat out, so it was out of the question for me with my penny. However, some very rich boys we knew were able to afford a boat, and they rowed round to the bank where we were waiting, and we boarded the boat as stowaways. It very nearly capsized with the extra weight and I did not enjoy it one bit, but I had to pretend that I did! Towards the end of the day races were organised. I was an excellent sprinter and always came away with a prize. My one penny spending money was spent on a bar of rock for my mother and dad. I could never resist sucking the end of it, so that when they

THERE'S NOTHING LIKE . . .

BIRD'S
CUSTARD
AND JELLIES

received it, it had been sucked to a point, and was covered with bits of grass!

The Congregational 'treat' was much more mundane. We boarded a bus and were taken to a field in Maghull, which boasted four swinging boats and a marquee. We still thought it wonderful, because you could eat as much as you liked, even though it was mostly buns, and everyone boasted they had had seven cups of tea.

About twice a year, mother went to her cousin's, who was very well off. Well, by our standards anyway; she lived in Mossley Hill and they had a bathroom! Her name was Maggie Baird, her husband was a master plumber and they had three children: Eugene, Florrie and Phyllis. Mother really went for the cast-offs and came home on the tram carrying bundles of them. Once she brought me back a lovely red and white checked dress, which actually fitted me. It had puffed sleeves and puffed pockets. Of course, I could only wear it on Sundays for church, but I felt like a princess. Then, joy of joys, one Monday, mother allowed me to go to school in it, to 'dirty it out'. It felt wonderful – suddenly, I was nearly as good as the others.

On rare occasions, mother took one of us, as a special treat, to Maggie Baird's. It certainly was a treat – we played in the garden, and paid frequent visits to the upstairs toilet. She had a beautiful, dark oak, Welsh dresser, with cream-coloured plates with blue polka dots arranged on them. We had scallops from the chip shop for tea and you could eat as much as you liked. When tea was over, I was ordered by my mother to help Florrie with the washing up. In this posh kitchen, Florrie began to run the water to wash the dishes. She kept running her hand up and down the water, and when I enquired why she was doing that, she replied, "I want it to come hot". As I watched, I could not believe my eyes. Magic! I now had a big secret, which I was going to surprise mother with when we got home. No more heavy pans and kettles on the fire – I would make the water hot! I ran the water for what seemed like ages, and it did not get hot and what's more, I had my ears boxed for wasting good water.

It was towards the end of summer when I next went to Mossley Hill, and Auntie Maggie asked if we liked loganberries. Never heard of them! She went into the garden and picked a bagful of these luscious fruits and we had them the next day for our tea, smothered in custard. A bit more upmarket than the rhubarb we were usually fed on.

Mother was the strong one in our family. She carried dad for the whole of their married life: seventy-three years. He 'hid' behind his deafness: "It's no use me going to the school/hospital/Town Hall. I wouldn't be able to hear." So mother did everything, including decorating, mending things, looking after the children, housework, shopping. She worked her socks off. She was either pregnant, or had just had a baby, for years, but she still kept plodding on.

Having a baby in those days meant being confined to bed for two weeks. During this time, known as her 'confinement', the new mother was not given ordinary food, but gruel, a type of weak porridge made with milk. The smell of the Valor oil stove, mixed with the smell of disinfectant, was a sure sign that mother was about to have yet another baby. A tense anxiety pervaded the house; dad wringing his hands and being commanded to put more pans and kettles of water on the fire, and bring up yet more newspapers. The midwife's bike in the yard, all shiny and new, with the strings stretched from the mudguards to the hub of the wheel, to keep her skirts away from the spokes. The elastic on the hem of her skirt, attached to her foot, to keep her skirt down and preserve her modesty, and the mysterious box on the back of the bike, which she carried upstairs with her. Did she bring the baby in that box? we asked ourselves as children. I recall going up to see mother when it was all over, and remarking how she looked very flushed. I was always terribly afraid that she would die in childbirth, and the relief I felt was wonderful. The new baby was secondary, it was just another red screamy thing in our already overcrowded house. However, I grew to love them all.

Doris aged twenty.

Mother had the last baby when I was nineteen. I was not even aware that she was pregnant. These things were never spoken of and I was very naive. 'Sex' was what coal was delivered in to Blundellsands households – that was the local joke. In the 1920s and 30s there was no sex education in schools and parents rarely told their children about the 'facts of life' - the subject was taboo. If a child entered a room when adults were talking, there would often be a stony silence, 'little pigs have big ears'. Our meagre knowledge was gained from sleazy remarks, like when a woman was obviously pregnant, 'we know what she's been up to!' Sex was dirty and sinful and only to be enjoyed by the male sex. Men 'sowed their wild oats' and were not quite men unless they had done so. Women were 'sluts' if they did, although they were the ones who bore the full consequence of their 'sins'. Some were incarcerated in mental homes, or convents, and were considered 'not quite nice' if they had a baby and were not married.

Most girls dreaded their wedding night because they were ignorant of what it entailed. The idea was that you endured it, it was your duty. In the cinema, the scene would show a young couple on their wedding night and he would discretely draw the curtains. The rest was left to the imagination. Many men were ignorant too. If they wished to purchase 'French letters', as they were called in those days, and a woman came to serve them, they would ask for a packet of razor blades instead! However, it was manly to pretend that you were knowledgeable about such things.

It has to be said that there were a few birth control clinics around. The first one was opened in Clarence Street and another in Linacre Mission, Litherland, but very few women used them. It would have been far too embarrassing to go to such a place and also, for many women, their conscience would prevent it, as birth control was against their religious beliefs. On one occasion Liverpool city council was asked to fund one of the clinics. They gave £100 for a year, and at the same time donated £500 for a single day's cricket match, showing where their priorities lay.

Women were raped, children sexually abused, but it was all kept under wraps. Such crimes were not reported. The word 'paedophile' was not used, they were just 'bad men' in our day.

One rather wonders how people managed to have sex in their small, over-crowded homes, but somehow they did. Was the desire for a bit of privacy

Doris (middle) aged thirty, at Butlins Pwllheli in 1949.

one reason for most parents' insistence on regular attendance at Sunday School? In the summer time I suppose that couples were able to make love out of doors, but winter must have presented many problems. There was no such thing as the back of a car then! The old saying 'where there's a will, there's a way' was very true. Somehow it all went on, in spite of setbacks.

Mother's last baby was born two months premature and was very sickly. I was allowed to name him and I called him Alan. He only lived for twenty-four hours. Mother, of course, was confined to bed, so I carried the baby downstairs, and laid him on the old couch, covering his tiny still white body with a piece of sheeting. I had no idea what would happen next, but soon a man in a navy blue suit arrived on a bike carrying a box. I knew at once what he had come for and I opened the door. He came in, put our dear little baby in the box, fastened it down, without uttering one word, wrapped the box in brown paper and string, and rode away with it under his arm. As I watched his retreating figure I dissolved into floods of tears. I was horrified that everyone would think that it was just a parcel being taken to the post office, but it was our baby. To this day that image still upsets me. Unable to afford a grave, baby Alan was buried beside a young mother who had died in childbirth, something that was all too common in those days.

After leaving school I worked as a glove machinist in Johnson's dry cleaners. From Monday to Friday we worked from 8am to 5.30pm, Saturday from 8am to 12 noon. In summer we had to work until 8pm and received no overtime pay and we had just one week's holiday per year. I was earning twenty-six shillings a week when I left in 1940.

By the time of the Munich Crisis in 1938, I had been courting a lad called Bill for eighteen months. He was a reservist in the Royal Navy and was called into service in July 1938. Two days before he had to report to *HMS Drake* in Plymouth, Bill called at our house at 7.30 in the morning and asked me to go to town with him. I was feeling really poorly, but worried that the outbreak of war was imminent and afraid that we would not see each other again for a long time, I agreed to go with him.

We boarded a Ribble bus at Seaforth, sixpenny return, and climbed to the upper deck. There, at 8.30 in the morning, he took my hand and asked me to marry him. I didn't know what to say — he liked a drink and my family was strictly teetotal. He was also a sailor — and everyone knew what sailors were like. However, I consented, and we went to Beaverbrooks, which was then in Church Street, and he bought me a three-stoned diamond ring for six pounds, fifteen shillings. I felt as though I was the only girl in the world with a diamond ring. My right hand became redundant! The war did not break out then, but Bill was away for six weeks.

In September 1939 the war really did begin. The early part of the war was called the 'Phoney War' as the public perception was that very little seemed to happen, but Bill's first ship was a minelayer, *HMS Adventure*, and was blown up as early as November 1939. He was given survivor's leave and was naturally annoyed when he heard people using this term, it certainly was not a phoney war at sea.

We were married in August 1940, just after the Dunkirk evacuation. The war had escalated to such an extent that we were waiting for Hitler to invade. At first we thought that we would have to cancel the wedding, as Bill's ship, a depot ship called *Hecla*, was due to sail, but the sailing date was delayed and the sympathetic captain gave him twenty-four hours leave. On our wedding morning he walked from Lime Street Station to Seaforth, and was back on Lime Street Station the next morning at 10am. I was in floods of tears as I waved him off.

The wedding took place at Wilson's Lane Methodist Church at 2.30pm. Bill was in uniform, with creases in his bell-bottoms and wearing the little white silk bow which sailors wore on their wedding day. The organ played *Because* and *I'll Walk Beside You* and friends showered us with confetti. I had no money to pay for a reception, but Bill was a millionaire, he had twenty-four pounds and with this he paid for the reception. Norman's the Caterers from South Road, Waterloo, provided the York ham salad, sherry trifle, French pastries, brown and white bread and butter and tea, all for two shillings and nine pence per head. The wedding cake was three pounds from Sayers. Bill paid five pounds for drinks for his family. My family were strictly teetotal and the disapproval showed on their faces.

We managed to escape from the reception to spend a precious couple of hours in my mother's sitting room, then went to Bill's sister's for the night. Our wedding night was disturbed by an air-raid, so we were embarrassed by having to spend time in the street shelter. No bombs were dropped but I was very frightened.

There was another painful goodbye as Bill returned to his ship the *Hecla*. My fears for his safety were soon realised when the *Hecla* was gas mined and several lives were lost, but thankfully, he was not among the casualties. The ship had been headed for East Africa, but had to be put in to South Africa to be repaired. The Second Front started and the ship was called to the Mediterranean. There, off Gibraltar, she was hit by six torpedoes, killing three hundred men. The first torpedo saved Bill's life, as it blew him clear of the ship. He was a very strong swimmer and was in the water for sixteen hours, before an American destroyer picked him up.

Letters sent home during the war were censored and often were full of holes where the censor had cut out any bits which were considered to be risky in any way and might have given the enemy important information. I was so relieved when the cable came, 'Safe and well. Don't write, see you soon. Love you a million billions. Bill.' He led a charmed life throughout the war. His next ship caught fire, but again, he lived to fight again.

Whenever my husband came home on leave it presented a problem. My mother's house was still over-crowded. My sister bought a bed-settee, which was kept in the sitting room, so that when her husband was on leave, they could sleep there. We could borrow it when my husband came home, but if they both came home together, we had to travel round relatives to find somewhere to stay. It worried us that we had nowhere to live if the war ended. Rented accommodation was very difficult to find, and we did not even know what the word 'mortgage' meant.

We were delighted when Kitty, my husband's sister, said she had asked her landlord if Bill and I could have the next house that became vacant. She was a very good tenant who paid regularly, so we too became tenants of the end

Doris and Bill were married while he was on twenty-four hours' leave from his ship the 'Hecla'. He was wearing the little white silk bow which sailors wore on their wedding day.

house in Chelsea Road. We didn't care what it was like, at least we would have somewhere to live when the war ended. It was 1943 when I moved in with my sister.

The house was in a terrible state. It had two bedrooms, a box room and a room which contained a bath, but no washbasin or toilet. The lavatory was at the bottom of the yard. It also had a sitting room, living room and kitchen. The rent was seven shillings and ninepence per week, which was all we could afford. I had had to give up my job at Johnsons as soon as I married, which was usual in many firms and I attained a job collecting for Wireless Services Ltd, on Stanley Road, until I was called up to do war work in 1941. I was given the choice of going into the forces or working on munitions. Anyone who was fit was forced to work during the war, but, in any case, the allotment from the Navy was too small to live on. I was in the ROF on shift work until the war ended in 1945.

I decided that the house had to be decorated. Of course, wallpaper was unobtainable, as was the labour to do the work. No men around – so we had to get on with it ourselves. I began to strip the paper (nine layers in all) off the sitting room wall and three quarters of the wall fell down! I rang the landlord, who responded with a solicitor's letter to say that he would sue me for damages to his property. In desperation, I ran to the Town Hall. I was in tears. I had visions of court proceedings and having to pay a large fine. The end result was that the council ordered him to repair the damage within a month, or they would do it, and charge him.

He sent round a couple of cowboys who, I am convinced, had never plastered a wall before in their lives. They left a huge bow in the wall and more mess than I had seen in my life. We cleaned it up, and then distempered the walls. We used a beige colour, then using little bits of sponge, we stippled it with greens and yellows. The effect was quite attractive.

Of course, we could not buy curtains, but blackout material could be obtained. We bleached it, then dyed it green. It was a bit streaky, but we put up with it. I bought a gas cooker from a saleroom for two pounds, even though the oven door would not close properly. I borrowed a kitchen table and bought four dining chairs from a neighbour for thirty-nine shillings.

When my husband came home on leave, we bought some brown linoleum from a shop in Walton Road. Of course, they could not deliver it, so my husband had to carry it for about two and a half miles, on his shoulder. Eventually, we were able to buy utility furniture, which was very plain, functional stuff. As we were limited as to how much of this we could buy, we just bought a dressing table, a wardrobe, a tallboy and a bed. I still have the tallboy, which is made of good solid wood. A permit was needed to purchase curtains and we were able to get enough for two windows.

The house was a complete disaster and I never liked it or felt at home there. It seemed that every few weeks the pipes burst, with water pouring through the ceilings, leaving ugly brown stains. The landlord was always very reluctant to rectify matters. "Can't get the labour," was his usual plea. We had to move into the sitting room, as we could not light the fire in the kitchen, and the fireplace smoked us out; we were permanently black with soot!

There was a brick boiler in the back kitchen in which I boiled my white laundry, using a dolly tub and dolly peg to get the clothes clean. The water was then used to swill the yard. We wasted nothing. Despite all these drawbacks, we lived in the house for twelve years, until we were able to exchange it for a nice council house, which we eventually bought, and we have now lived in it for forty-five years.

By today's standards, I had a very deprived childhood, but of the eleven children in our family, ten survived, and I am very proud of all of them. They are all good, hardworking citizens, they are all intelligent, in spite of all the deprivation we suffered.

May I add that I now have a polished oak dresser, with plates on. Alas, I never could find any plates decorated with those blue polka dots …

The stirrup pump was used after an air-raid to put out fires caused by incendiary bombs dropped by enemy aircraft to light up their targets.

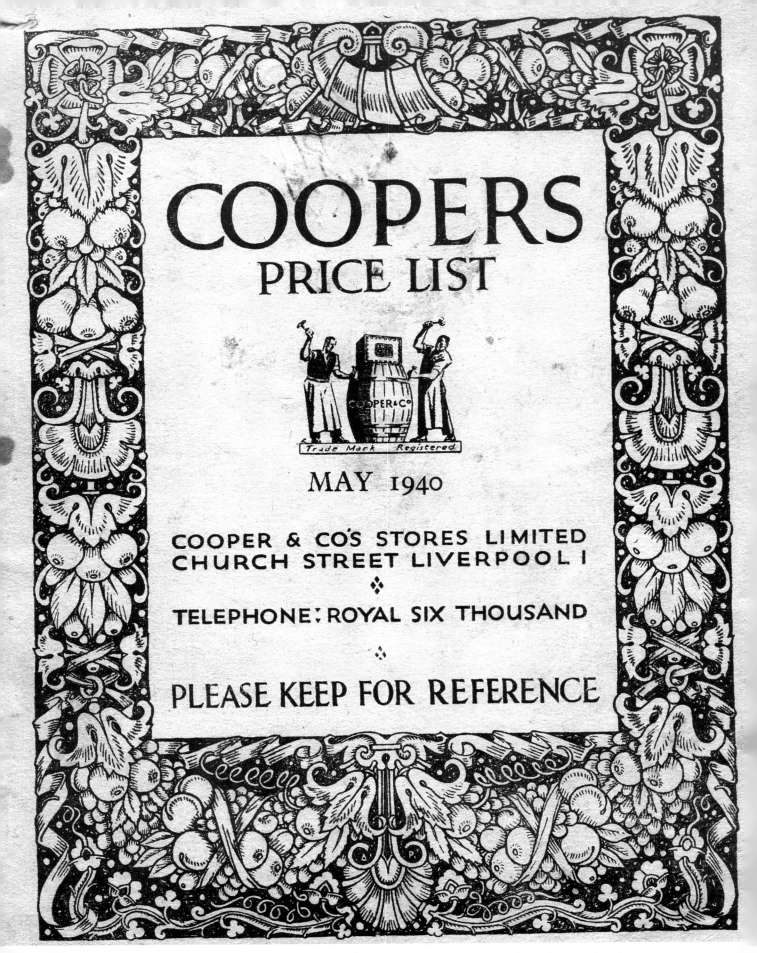

COOPERS
PRICE LIST

MAY 1940

COOPER & CO'S STORES LIMITED
CHURCH STREET LIVERPOOL 1

❖

TELEPHONE: ROYAL SIX THOUSAND

❖

PLEASE KEEP FOR REFERENCE

Lil Otty – Born 1919

I was born in Everton, Liverpool, as were my parents, on 29 October 1919, the first girl of a family of three brothers. The eldest was sixteen, the next thirteen and my youngest brother was just four years old. He was not too pleased when he first found that he had a sister, but we were close throughout our adult lives. Two other brothers had died before I was born. My sister was born two years and seven months after me and was an extremely delicate baby. I was told that she was just over a pound in weight, and had to be washed in olive oil and wrapped in cotton wool. There were no clothes to fit her, and she had to be carried around on a pillow. With none of today's modern equipment, only the patience of a good mother, she has reached the age of seventy-nine and is in good health.

My father was in the Royal Engineers in the First World War, and served on the trains transporting the wounded soldiers back from the front; a non-combatant role as he refused to carry or use a gun. My mother held the fort back at home by taking over his job in a bread shop. After the war my father took up his job again and by the 1930s was the manager of a bread shop in Great Homer Street. He would walk up and down the hilly streets of Everton clutching his Gladstone bag containing the shop's takings, so that he could work on the cash books until the early hours of the morning each weekend. Every Saturday, as children, we would take his dinner down the hill to the shop, as it did not close until 9pm. My father eventually retired from work through ill health and never worked again. Fortunately, my mother was a born survivor, with enormous inner strength. Both her parents had died when she was young; her mother when she was twelve and her father when she was sixteen. She went to work in a doctor's surgery in Rodney Street, met my father, and married at twenty-one years of age. She made a home for her two younger brothers when they came out of the Bluecoat School.

The small street in Everton where I was born had just six houses in it, with odd numbers from one to eleven. We looked out onto the back of a row of other houses and there was a quarry at the end of the street, which made mortar for an adjoining builder's yard on Wye Street, with the main office in Mere Lane. The land was later used by the Gas Company but its premises have since been demolished and a community centre now occupies the site.

Cooper's magnificent provisions shop on Church Street was a local landmark, although the items which were sold there were out of the reach of many of Liverpool's poorer citizens.

The " NEW DEFIANCE."

Built with best quality British fittings throughout, flanged chain wheel, transport chain, Brook's Plyflex saddle, brazed handlebar lugs, Villier's freewheel. Complete with basket, Brook's tool bag and tools.
C1380/11206   With Dunlop Clipper Carrier Tyres and Bluemel's Reflector **£7 7 0**

Cycling was an inexpensive and popular way of getting about, once you had bought your bike. Lil's brothers could not afford to buy new ones and so made their own from spare parts obtained from scrapyards. Lil longed to be given a ride, but was forbidden to do so by her mother.

We lived with the relentless noise of the grinding machine in the quarry and the steam engines delivering their loads, as well as the gentler sound of the shire horses clattering to and from the builder's yard with their heavy loads of bricks. The carters in charge of these transports were an integral part of our neighbourhood and knew each of us children by name and where we lived. They would ask for water to make tea in their enamel tea cans. As well as the constant noise, a perpetual haze of dust and grit rained down on our homes, making cleaning an ongoing battle, for which we received no apology or compensation.

The properties were eventually compulsorily cleared when they were a hundred years old, as they still had no indoor toilets or hot water systems. We were moved out, and one day the men arrived to strip the slates from the roofs, then a bulldozer came on the scene. Soon our homes were reduced to piles of rubble, being picked over by the rag and bone men. This was all done with little consideration for people's feelings and families and neighbours were scattered far and wide. But all this was to come much later – for now, back to my childhood.

We all attended church three times on Sunday and after church we visited our aunt and uncle in Netherfield Road. They had no family of their own, but brought up three families in a double-fronted house. The delicious smell of home baking and dinner cooking on the open range always filled their home. My uncle always gave us two pence each as we were leaving, but we were not allowed to spend it on a Sunday. Instead, we were encouraged to put it into the collection box for the church offering. I can still recall the distinctive sound of the pennies dropping into the collection box, against a backdrop of rousing hymns. After Sunday School we would go for a walk around Stanley Park. On arriving home the tea would be ready and friends would come to the house and share in the meal. The Wall's ice-cream man - 'Stop me and buy one' - would call and sit down for a cup of tea and a piece of pie. Father would treat us to a triangular block of ice-cream, but would not let us buy sweets. On Wednesdays we would have to queue up for a halfpenny pocket money.

Growing up in Everton, like all my contemporaries, I caught many childhood diseases. At seven I had rheumatic fever, and at fourteen, scarlet fever, both very serious illnesses at the time. I lost count of the number of times I had tonsillitis, but, with good nursing from my mother, I survived them all.

Cycling was a relatively inexpensive way of getting about when I was young and I longed to ride a bicycle, but my mother had forbidden me to accept any offers of rides from my brothers. They had built their own bikes from spare parts obtained from scrapyards, until they could afford new ones. They used them to get to work and to cycle to North Wales at the weekends. Cycling accidents involving pedestrians were not uncommon and I was twice knocked over by a bike. The first time my hair became entangled in the spokes of the wheel and left me minus a ringlet. The second time I escaped with bruising, but the cyclist was thrown to the ground.

But my longing for a bike was undiminished and in my teens my opportunity finally came when a friend asked me to borrow a neighbour's bike so that we could go for a ride. We set off early on a Sunday morning, having to stop now and then for a rest, when suddenly disaster struck; I fell off and sprained my ankle. My next trip was with a boyfriend, who became so annoyed with me for being so slow that he cycled on ahead; I was only in Seaforth when he had arrived in Hightown and he passed me on his way home! I decided that I was not a natural cyclist and went back to Shanks's pony.

I attended Lorraine Street Elementary School from the age of five until I was fourteen, where I enjoyed swimming at Margaret Street baths and also loved playing rounders in the schoolyard. I was also allowed to go on the school's flat roof to exercise with Indian dumb-bells.

I had a particular talent for sewing, quite an important part of the curriculum in those days, and one teacher would give me bits of mending to do, as I was very handy with a needle. So, making up my mind about the job I wanted to do was no trouble, as sewing had always come first. My first job was in the sewing room of a small dressmakers in Coopers Building, Church Street, in Liverpool city centre and my meagre wage was five shillings and sixpence a week. There were three experienced workers and one junior who had to show me the ropes. In the early stages of my apprenticeship it was a case of, 'go for this and go for that, pick up pins, pass me so and so, make the tea, wash the cups, keep the room tidy, brush and mop the floor before going home.'

Then I progressed to threading needles for the ladies, and small jobs such as sewing on buttons and hooks and eyes, or unpicking articles for repair. Some days I was given a sample of material or a button or buckle to match up with the sample. There were several stores to go round, large and small; the oldest in Lord Street, Frisby Dykes, and the large department stores such as Owen Owens in Clayton Square and Lewis's, Ranelaigh Street.

Some lunchtimes I used to go with some friends of my mother's to a café in Tarleton Street, where I paid sixpence for a dinner, sweet and a cup of tea. My working hours were 8.30am – 6.00pm, Monday to Friday. Saturday was supposed to be half day, but nearly every week it would be 4pm before we were allowed to go home. I had to wait for garments to be finished, then set off to the parcel post along Park Lane from where they were delivered to the customer. I received the sum of five-shillings and sixpence, with no overtime. I liked the ladies there, but not the workroom, it was too small and cramped.

The first time I was sent out with a sample and account card to purchase material, I walked round and round the outside of Owen Owens, too embarrassed to go in and ask, because I had not been given any actual money to purchase the item. I eventually plucked up courage, went in, and spoke to the assistant, who right away put me at my ease, "That's all right, dear. You have an account card with us". I was so relieved, a good job I had not panicked and jumped on the first tram home!

I only stayed in my first job for three months, leaving to start at an overall factory on Edge Lane for a shilling more – six shillings and sixpence a week. I had to do several jobs before ending up working on a sewing machine. I was prevented from learning how to operate the power machine for two years due to poor eyesight. I had to attend a specialist clinic in Rodney Street for treatment of a squint in my left eye. At first I was a clerk in the machine room office, then the printing room, where I enjoyed fixing the printing type and operating the machine which printed the tickets for garments finished in the machine room.

In the late thirties, people of the working class never dreamed of holidays abroad. If they went anywhere, it was more likely to be Moreton over on the Wirral, or Rhyl in North Wales. My first holiday with my work pals started once the Easter holidays were over and the sunny days finally appeared. On our way home from work we would spend ages planning how we could scrape the cash together to pay for this escape from the city and into the country for a bit of fresh air. We decided on walking either to or from work. The saving could be up to sixpence a day if the weather was fine and we could walk both ways. We aimed at saving ten shillings each for the week away. We all made a new dress as well as altering the ones we already had.

The first year, for myself, but the second for some of my friends, was in a bungalow, a wooden affair on top of a hill, near a place called Garth. About eight of us travelled by train to Ruabon then caught a local bus to avoid carrying our heavy cases, stuffed with food and clothes, up the steep hill. The railway porters greeted us with huge smiles; they remembered my pals who had travelled there the previous year. We smiled back – we were all in high spirits, ready for our holiday.

For Lil and her friends,
the holidays they shared together in
Garth, in Wales, provided some of their
happiest memories. The September after
these photos were taken, war broke out and
their lives were changed forever.

After arriving and settling in and deciding who was sharing with whom, the next thing was to sort out rotas for the various jobs which would have to be done. There was cooking, setting the table, washing up, shopping during the week, bed-making, fetching water and keeping the place tidy. Then there was the emptying of the slops, because the toilet, or WC as it was called then, was some way from the bungalow.

We would walk, arm in arm, chattering and laughing into Llangollen and back again, dawdling along the canal tow-path looking for wild flowers. We had no trouble making our own fun by playing rounders or other such games. The weather was scorching hot and we basked in the sun, young and happy in each other's company, without a care in the world – but also without a cover over our heads! Two of us were fair-skinned, so we were cooked to a frazzle, our first lesson in the hazards of sunbathing. I have never tried it since.

We all loved dancing and we spent hours practising the latest steps, inside the bungalow and out in the grounds. At night we held quizzes or played card games – whist and snap – singing the latest hit songs as we played. Sometimes a couple of local chaps would call around to share our company and we would all act silly, holding mock weddings and dressing up.

We all enjoyed that holiday so much: the company, the beautiful countryside and the glorious weather. It was my first taste of independence and I loved the close friendship and the way we all helped each other with the chores. As soon as the holiday was over and we were back in Liverpool, we started planning our return visit the following year. And so, after months of expectation and hard saving, we found ourselves once more on the little local bus, chugging up that same, familiar hillside, giggling and chattering and full of excitement, ready to do it all again.

But that was to be the last holiday we would spend together; our lives were about to be turned upside down. That September, after weeks of uncertainty, the Prime Minister, Neville Chamberlain, announced that we were at war with Germany. Before long, we all had to leave our jobs, called up for war work which separated us, some of us never to meet again. But I am still in touch with one friend. We still meet and enjoy our time together, although her health is not always good. Our friendship remains the same after seventy years.

When war broke out I was called up and sent to Automatic Telephone Manufacturers (Marconi), Edge Lane, where I became a stock clerk in a tool stores. I stayed in the job for thirteen years, enjoying the work and the company. My duties involved keeping the stock up-to-date and allowing extra delivery time because of the petrol rationing.

Many people, in the days following the declaration of war on 3 September, were forced to leave their homes or places of work to join the Armed Forces, or be considered for war work in factories. The majority of men and women had never travelled very far, even around their own towns. They lived in tight-knit communities, with their families and friends all around them.

Anxious mothers had to decide whether to send their children away as evacuees to the countryside. It was no easy thing for them to hand over their children's care to complete strangers, in remote and inaccessible places. They tried to present a calm exterior to ease the situation for their children, whilst inwardly they must have been consumed with worry. Their minds in turmoil, they had to face the practical problems involved in preparing the children for evacuation; clothes and belongings to be packed – a change of clothing would be the most one could own – a pillowcase used in place of an suitcase.

Lil looking very elegant in this studio portrait.

Lil did not marry the boy next door, but Stan did live in the next street. They married in 1952, when Lil was thirty-two.

They also had to deal with the emotional trauma of separation, as well as preparing them for a train journey, something few of them would ever have experienced.

Men, young enough and fit enough, were being called upon for recruitment into either the Army, the Navy, or the Air Force, where they faced stern discipline from sergeant majors and officers alike. They also had to rapidly learn all the skills they would need to make effective fighters. The women were next, being encouraged to opt for the Land Army, or to work in engineering or munitions factories, or any job which was previously undertaken by the male population. So there was an entire, nationwide movement of people leaving home, not of their own choice.

After the war, some families had no homes to return to. With the main wage earners conscripted, wives were left to keep the home fires burning! And their contribution was vital; they took on many jobs such as fire wardens, ambulance and tram drivers. Women took over during the war, particularly during the air-raids. Day after day they would leave their homes to go shopping, then struggle to cobble a decent meal together for growing families on the meagrest of rations. They would make soups from marrow bone, rabbit, chicken or ox tail, and scouse was a tasty way to eke out a meagre meat ration. If no meat was available, blind scouse would be made from potatoes, turnips, carrots and cabbage – the only vegetables which were readily available. Salt fish was popular and cheap with bread pudding, a nutritious and filling pudding. They did a splendid job, with very little appreciation for a situation they could not walk away from. These women and men were the backbone of the country, loyal and true citizens.

I married after the war in 1952 when I was thirty-two, to Stan, whom I had known well since childhood, as he had lived in the next street to me. There was no engagement ring – money was still very tight. The men in the stores had a surprise when I announced the day of the wedding – they had the oak shelf in the making! I was lucky enough to be able to continue in my job, due to an expansion of the type of work I did. Post-war women usually had to return to their previous place of work, as their jobs had to be given back to the soldiers returning from the war in 1945.

Now the old neighbourhood where I grew up has virtually disappeared and I am left a stranger in my own locality. On the day our street was demolished the memories came floating back – I caught a glimpse of our old wallpaper and remembered the day my brother was teasing me and I threw a cup of Ovaltine towards him and it splattered all over the newly-decorated kitchen wallpaper. The cupboard with nothing left in it, the fireplace, cold and choked with rubble, with no more potato cakes to be baked. The front door thrown on the scrapheap after being kicked and opened countless times a day. The steps no more to be lovingly cleaned with sandstone from the cemetery by proud housewives on their hands and knees. The old lamppost that we used to swing around on a piece of rope ... all gone.

The clouds of dust finally settled and I turned my back on a life which has gone but is not forgotten – just memories. Those of us who have survived the past have placed their hopes for the future in the generations to come.

The heart was torn out of the old neighbourhoods around Scotland Road in the 1960s – leaving only memories.

Vera Jeffers – Born 1925

I was born in 1925, in Ruskin Street, Walton, in my grandmother's house; my parents had lived there with her since they married in 1917. My first memories, however, are of my home in Trouville Road, Anfield, which was a council house. It had a parlour, a living room and a kitchen. Built just after the First World War, it had three bedrooms, a bathroom upstairs and gardens back and front. We were very lucky to have such a house. It probably had something to do with my father being a disabled ex-service man, and living in over-crowded conditions. My brother was born there when I was four years old.

My father had come home from the war in 1916, unfit for further service. His lungs and eyes had been badly damaged by gas. He had been in the Territorials, and so was conscripted immediately the war began, serving with the Liverpool 5th Kings Regiment. His war pension amounted to eight shillings and three pence per week, but in 1918, it was suddenly stopped. It was proved however, that he was still a sick man and the pension was restored. Then, at the beginning of 1921, he was sent for another medical, and a few days later received a stark letter, which stated: 'the temporary aggravation of your disability as the result of National Service has passed away'. That was it, even though he was still a sick man, his pension was stopped again, this time for good.

A printer by trade, my father eventually returned to his job when he was able to. But in 1922, many businesses had started to lay off men because of the Depression and my father lost his job. I still have the reference his employer gave: 'He is an industrious worker, and very willing, and we can thoroughly recommend him, and his workmanship is all that can be desired.' But his wartime injuries had ruined his health, and during his post-war working life he was always in and out of hospital.

He never recovered his good health and died when I was six and my brother only nineteen months old. We were staying with my grandmother at the time, so that my mum could stay at the hospital with dad. Gran had made a bed for us with cushions and pillows, on the floor of the alcove in her room. I remember the time vividly, because it was New Year's Eve 1931. Terry

The German bombers ripped the heart out of Liverpool city centre. Still a teenager, Vera was caught in the middle of one of the worst bombing raids of the war, and had to make her way back from town to Norris Green, clambering over rubble and often having to run for shelter as the sirens repeatedly screamed out their warning.

At the age of ten Vera had this special photograph taken to commemorate the Silver Jubilee of George V.

and I were unable to sleep because people were singing loudly in the street below. Then my mother came into the room and I could not understand why she was crying when everyone else seemed to be so happy.

There was no such thing as sick leave in those days, if you were continually off sick you were sacked and someone else got your job, usually for less pay. Unemployment was very high and very few men could find permanent work on their return home from the war. Many of them had no regular employment at all until the start of the Second World War. Most young people leaving school could find work but, more often than not, they would be sacked before they were eligible for full pay at the age of twenty-one. Even those who were apprenticed would have to leave once their training was finished and would have to look for work elsewhere.

We stayed at gran's for a while after my father died, and then returned home to find it had been broken into. It was dark when we arrived and I remember how frightened and bereft we felt when we found the front door wide open. Our fears were intensified by the thunderous sound of a runaway horse, which came wildly galloping down the street. Apparently it had escaped from the field at the back of the houses. Our good neighbour, hearing our cries, came to our assistance and we stayed the night in her house.

I started school when I was five years old at All Saints, Anfield. I have no particular memories of this school, except that I did not like it, and cried bitterly every time I had to go. My mother dragged me there every morning and afternoon. The desks were the kind that held about ten children each, all sitting alongside each other on the attached bench, row upon row. We had slates and chalk and counting rails, and these were put to good use. Not much play went on in the classroom in those days.

Whenever we stayed with gran, I always felt secure and safe. When we woke in the morning there was always a little surprise for us, a piece of fruit maltloaf spread with marmalade, or half an apple each or perhaps a few sultanas in twists of paper. Grandma's kitchen was the cosiest, most comforting place I knew. The shelf in the corner was full of stone jars in which she stored her homemade remedies. There were also bottles of tonic wine, which she made with beetroot and Guinness. She always gave a bottle of this to anyone recovering from illness, or pregnancy. As a child, I was often given a glass of it too, supposedly to improve my appetite which was poor. Often when we were sick with some childish ailment, we would lie on gran's old horsehair sofa wrapped up in her black shawl in front of the fire. Many a toothache was eased with a clove to bite on, or an earache soothed with warm olive oil. A sore throat was treated with a drop of Friar's Balsam on a cube of sugar, which we were given to suck. When the time came for us to go home, we never ever left gran's empty-handed. There would be a cake or pie that she had made, or some dinner for Mum to warm up the next day.

Soon after my father died we left Trouville Road; mother could never settle there and the break-in only made things worse. The rent too, was more than she could afford, she only had her widow's pension of ten shillings a week, plus five for me and three for my brother. We moved to a cheaper house in Norris Green, on a new estate built purposely to re-house people from the terrible slums in the inner city. But the new tenants found that their rent had almost doubled. Few families could afford it, so many of them moved back to their old neighbourhoods. Norris Green was also a completely different environment from the one they were used to; there was no corner shop where women could get 'tick' to tide them over until pay-day, and there were no pawnshops either. Countless families depended on such places to eke out what little money they had to live on.

For the men, who were mostly dockers, it meant a longer journey to the docks and 'pen', and the hope of work. As far as I know, the pen was not an enclosure of any kind, just a specific place on the dock road, usually in close proximity to each dock gate. Dockers were employed on a casual basis at that time, so the men would assemble and wait to be chosen by the clerks of the various shipping companies. It was not unusual for a man to work for two or three different companies in a week and consequently have to collect the wages due to him from each separate company's office. Some men travelled by bike and some by 'shanks's pony'. What little they earned, if they were lucky enough to get work, barely covered their household expenses. These men also missed their local pubs, which were on virtually every corner in the old neighbourhoods, but were few and far between in Norris Green. Most families found Norris Green to be a bleak, unfriendly place to live. Some people jokingly called it 'debtors' retreat'.

While we lived there I attended St Teresa's infant school. This was a new school and everything in it was brand new. We had desks with lids, two children for each desk, and we each had a chair. It was a lovely school and I was happy while I was there. My school friends lived near me and we spent many happy hours playing in the street. Most street games had their own particular season, so consequently we were never bored.

We lived only a short walk away from the countryside, where there were meadows full of wild flowers. St Teresa's held its annual sports day in one of these meadows, in Oak Lane, now part of a vast private housing estate. There were the usual egg and spoon and sack races, and a couple of boxing bouts; our school produced some very good boxers. A few became quite well known in later years; Frank Hope and Eddie Pye, to name just two of them. We also had other competitions such as recitation, singing and dancing. I decided to enter for the latter on one occasion, intending to do a dance I had learned from a friend who had dancing lessons: *The Passing of Salome*. I had no ballet shoes, only a pair of pumps. Mother made me a costume out of an old net curtain, which comprised a pair of baggy trousers nipped in at the ankle, a bra-type top and a head-dress. This was a stiff band of yellow cardboard with a length of net curtain attached to the back of it and the ends fastened to my wrists. I just wore a pair of knickers underneath.

The day of the competition finally came and there I stood in all my splendour, when in walked Sister Magdalene. She took one look at me and nearly had a fit. "Get dressed immediately and cover yourself up, girl. Have you no shame?" she bawled. My costume, it seems, was immodest and had upset the nun's religious sensibilities, so I was forced to perform the dance in my ordinary clothes, which did nothing for my portrayal of Salome. I was very upset about it. The nuns were always very keen on modesty. We were

Remember When ...

Home Remedies

- Sulphur powder for a bad throat.
- Sulphur and treacle for the blood or skin blemishes.
- Soap mixed with sugar to draw a boil, draw out a splinter, or clear infection.
- Bread poultice for quinsy and other infections.
- Peroxide for ear troubles and also to clean wounds.
- Cinder tea for babies' wind (a piece of red hot cinder was dropped into water, which was then sieved and given to the baby).
- Hot salt to ease pain.
- Vinegar and brown paper for a headache.
- Camphorated oil or goose grease for a bad chest.
- Bicarbonate of soda for indigestion.
- Gentian violet for sores, warts and scabies (the 'itch').
- Iodine for general cuts and sores.

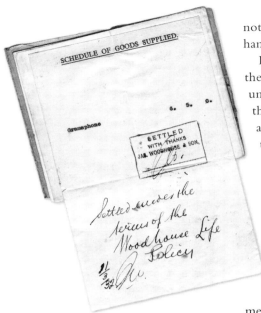

The final receipt for Vera's mother's beloved gramophone, which she had paid for over a period of fourteen months. She was ordered to sell the gramophone by the dreaded Mr Jones, a Public Assistance official, who in those days had the power to scrutinise every purchase made by those receiving benefit, forcing them to sell any item which was not deemed absolutely vital.

not allowed to tuck our skirts in the leg of our knickers, or to stand on our hands, or do 'crabby'; innocent activities that my friends and I enjoyed.

Like many of our neighbours, we were on Public Assistance. These were the days of the means test and a very close watch was kept on those unfortunate people who depended on it. You never knew when Mr Jones the PA man would call. He had eyes like a hawk and never missed a thing, always on the lookout for some item in the home that could be sold and the proceeds used to live on. Mr Jones ordered my mother to sell our gramophone, which was her pride and joy. It broke our hearts to see it go. It was the kind that had to be wound up by a handle at the side and we always had to give it an extra wind half way through the record, otherwise it would run down and the music sound all strange and drawly. We did not have a wireless, so the loss of the gramophone was awful. Our favourite records then were *Tip Toe through the Tulips*, and the scary one about Anne Bolyn: *With her head tucked underneath her arm, she walked the Bloody Tower.*

These were hard times and folk did whatever they could to make ends meet. There were some enterprising people, however, who started up small businesses in their own homes. Some would buy a small stock of cigarettes, a few loaves of bread, sugar, tea, etc, just to accommodate neighbours who had run short of these commodities. It saved a long trek to the shops, and it was also very convenient when the shops were shut. One woman sold homemade cakes, and there was a man who made plant tables out of wooden orange boxes that he bought for a couple of pence from the local greengrocer. After smoothing and varnishing the wood, these tables looked quite presentable and many a house had an Aspidistra in the front window on one of Joe's tables.

Another member of this black economy was the woman who cooked and sold chips at lunchtime, two or three days a week. There would always be a couple of women and children, with their basins covered with a clean cloth or newspaper, waiting outside her back door for the chips to cook. This lady had a very narrow escape one day when Mr Jones almost caught her. Luckily, someone had spied him at the top of the road and quickly passed the warning on. There was such a scramble and within seconds chip pan and basins had disappeared, hidden under the privet hedge in the garden. Someone stood guard while tea towels, 'pinnies' and aprons were frantically used to fan away the lovely smell of the chips.

We would have been much worse off without the support and help we received from our relations. They would buy us much needed clothes or shoes whenever they could afford to, and often a big jar of malt and cod-liver oil, which was not as obvious as clothes and went unnoticed hidden under a pan on the shelf in the kitchen. It had a soft, toffee-like consistency and was designed to make it easier for a child to take the important vitamins contained in cod-liver oil. It was an aid to nutrition, rather than a medicine and was used to supplement a poor diet.

If we went out anywhere, mum walked us miles out of our way and would not go by tram or bus if we were wearing anything new, just in case we met Mr Jones. If by chance he did see us, he would be at our house the next day demanding to know where the new clothes came from. The penalty was a cut in benefit money for a few weeks. There was always the possibility that gran, and my aunt, would be expected to make a regular contribution towards our keep. I was always very much aware that these things upset my mother immensely. Mr Jones was my childhood 'bogey man' and his memory has stayed with me all of my life.

The St Vincent de Paul Society, still in action today, from the local Catholic Church, was always very good to the poor. They would sometimes give my mum a much needed 'couple of bob' to buy some extra food or other necessities. The Masonic Society was also kind to us. A family friend was a member of the Masons, and through him we were invited to the children's Christmas party, or a day out in the summertime.

Eventually we moved house again and went to live over a shop in Aintree, to be nearer gran. The rent was twelve shillings per week – a huge amount out of her eighteen and sixpence income. I hated living in that house, it was so dark and miserable; the only access was from the back entry and up the long dark yard, and it was on a very busy road, so we either had to play in the yard, or go to Aintree Park. But my mother's friend, who lived nearby, was a very good pianist and we had some very happy times with her and her family. The song, *The Dark Town Strutters Ball,* was popular then and Molly could make anyone's feet tap once she got going at the piano.

The move meant yet another school for me and my brother – the Blessed Sacrament School in Walton Vale. This was another old building. The door of our classroom opened directly onto the playground, which was covered with cinders. There was a row of toilets at the bottom of the yard with a wall in front. The toilet doors had a large gap at the top and bottom. I tried desperately not to go during school time, because some of the boys used to run through the toilet passageway, pushing the doors open as they went, which could be embarrassing. Also, if you asked to leave the room in class, you had to take a piece of paper from a string hanging by the classroom door, which was also hugely embarrassing.

In the 1930s a special visiting permit was required before relatives could visit anyone in hospital. In cases of contagious diseases, no visitors were allowed.

For those on low incomes, paying the rent left little money for other necessities.

Early in 1935 there was a very serious epidemic of diphtheria, which killed many children, including one of my school friends. The usual symptoms of this disease are a high temperature, fever and a heavy discharge from the nose. The throat is very inflamed to begin with and then a white, patchy skin starts to grow over it, impairing breathing. I remember the doctor taking a swab from my throat and the next thing the dreaded fever van arrived. This was a box-like van, made of wood and painted dark green. I seem to recall that the back part, where the patient was put, was windowless. The dark green colour distinguished it from the ordinary ambulance, which as far as I can remember, was either varnished wood, or painted in a light colour. Delirious and terrified, I was transported to Sparrowhall, the Fever Hospital, at Fazackerly. I was in hospital for ten weeks and visitors were not allowed, even on my tenth birthday, so I did not see my mother again until I was discharged. Missing her was even more traumatic than the illness itself. I was finally due to go home after seven weeks in hospital, when a new patient was found to have scarlet

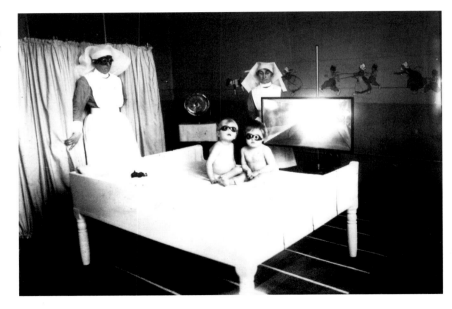

Poor diet often led to deficiencies in crucial vitamins and minerals. Vitamin D deficiency led to a condition called rickets, in which the bones soften and become deformed. These tots are being treated for rickets by exposing them to artificial sunlight.

fever, another serious illness of those times. The whole ward was quarantined for another three weeks.

Another childhood complaint in those days, which you rarely hear of now, was rickets, caused by vitamin D deficiency, due to a poor diet. My brother developed rickets and had to spend over twelve months in a convalescent home in Heswall. He was a very sickly child and was often in and out of hospital. As well as rickets, he suffered very badly with recurring TB abscesses on his neck, which kept him away from school for quite long periods, when he was taken into Alder Hey Hospital on three separate occasions. He was also taken into Walton Hospital with measles, and another time into Netherfield Road Hospital with scarlet fever. Bad health dogs him still; he now has multiple sclerosis. My mother always used to put his poor health down to her long, painful confinement; he was a ten month baby and weighed in at twelve and a half pounds. She had him at home, with only a midwife in attendance, who, according to my mother, kept telling her to stop crying and get on with it.

Whooping cough, measles and mumps were also common. If you had whooping cough, you would be taken down to the nearest 'cocky watchman's' hut and held over his hot tar bucket to breathe in the fumes, which were supposed to ease the terrible racking, choking cough. People had great faith in this bizarre remedy, and it did seem to help in most cases.

On the day that I was discharged from hospital, I discovered to my huge surprise, that my mother was getting married again. Not having seen her for ten weeks, I knew nothing about it. A strange woman came to collect me from the hospital, and I was taken to a house in Norris Green, which turned out to be my new home. I arrived in time for the second sitting at the wedding breakfast, which we had in the house. I was introduced to my new stepbrothers and sisters, there now being two boys and a girl older than I was, and two girls and a boy younger, I was no longer the oldest. My stepfather turned out to be my Uncle Tom, who used to come and visit us every Friday night. I made friends very quickly with my new siblings, though the whole affair seemed rather strange and puzzling to a ten-year-old.

Later that same day, the lady who had collected me from hospital returned and this time I was taken to a convalescent home, miles away in Freshfield, where I was to stay for two weeks. No one gave me any explanation of the day's events and I went away feeling utterly miserable, upset and unwanted. The old adage in those days was, 'children should be seen and not heard', a philosophy which resulted in much emotional cruelty. We were expected to accept, without question, everything that happened to us.

My stepfather was the man in charge of the pen, at the docks. He was the one who picked the men for work each day, so we often had women coming to our house begging him to give their son or husband work the next day, more often than not, because of some family crisis, such as a sick child and they could not afford a doctor. There was no National Health Service then, you paid to see a doctor, and also for any medication. This was often beyond the means of the poor, who mostly used the dispensary at the hospital where, for sixpence, you explained the symptoms of the sick person to the dispenser, and would be given a bottle of medicine or some tablets.

My stepfather had a regular job and wage but it was still barely enough to keep two adults and seven children. My mother sat by the fire each night darning socks, patching sheets and the boys' trousers. Every boy, and often men too, had patched trousers. Boys wore short trousers until they left school, often with more patches than the original material they were made of. Mother was skilled at renovating and sewing; able to make an old dress or coat look brand new. My stepfather mended our shoes and cut our hair, but he charged my mother for doing it! He considered it part of her general household expenses. He would generously give money to one of the women who came to him pleading for their men's jobs, but my mother had to manage on a strict budget, and had to account for every penny she spent.

I enjoyed having brothers and sisters, though we did have many a squabble. We each had jobs to do around the house, particularly the girls. I got on well with my stepbrother, Billy, who was about twelve months older than I was. He made a cart out of some old wood and four old pram wheels. We had to go to the Co-op (the 'Co'ee', we called it) for the groceries every Saturday morning, and having the cart made it a lot easier and much more fun. Very often the wheels buckled, and we would go round the neighbours asking if they had any old ones that they didn't want, often ending up with a lopsided cart.

I was always stage struck when I was young and when I was twelve, I auditioned for a pantomime without telling my mother and was offered a job. I would get my keep, travelling expenses and five shillings a week. I would need a navy velour coat and hat with a badge and black ankle band shoes. We always had plain, no-nonsense, lace-up shoes, one pair a year, and they had to last until the following year. There were ructions when my mother found out about all this and she refused to let me go. She could not buy such luxuries for me and not the other children. Big arguments followed, but I eventually won the day because, after all, I would be earning

Without her mother's permission, and using impressive initiative for a twelve-year-old, Vera auditioned for, and was given, a part in a pantomime which played at the Lyceum, Sheffield, for fourteen weeks.

five shillings a week. It was arranged that I could keep sixpence and the rest would be sent home to help pay for my new things.

So off I went to the Lyceum Theatre in Sheffield, to appear in *Mother Goose* as one of Eileen Rogan's Twelve Little Rosebuds. The pantomime ran for fourteen wonderful weeks, during which time I met some of the stars of the day; Rex Harrison and Michael Redgrave, to name but two. Dora Bryan was also an Eileen Rogan girl, but I didn't meet her, she was in the Manchester group. While in Sheffield, we went to school each day except for Wednesday afternoons, when there was a matinee, and of course we were celebrities among the other schoolchildren who gathered round for our autographs. We were invited to parties and teas, and wherever we went we had an escort with us. We could not go anywhere on our own because of the 'white slave traffic'. I had no idea what this meant, but I learned later that they were people who abducted young girls. But I was unconcerned, just happy to be there. I wanted to take the stage up as a career but the war put an end to all my plans.

Back in Liverpool, after being a duffer for most of my schooldays, I began to pick up and did quite well once I reached St Teresa's senior school. Our teachers were strict, and we respected them. I was given the cane sometimes for minor misdemeanours such as being late for school, running along the corridor, talking in class and untidy work, but I don't think it did any of us any harm. It was instilled in us that we could not always do as we liked, rules had to be obeyed. We were taught to have respect for other people, and also ourselves. I really loved my school and the teachers, and I was very sad when the day came for me to leave.

I was fourteen years old when the war started, and about to leave school. I had been married for fourteen months by the time it came to an end. Those six years in between were my teenage years, wholly occupied with the events and happenings of wartime Britain.

As Norris Green, on the outskirts of the city, was considered to be a relatively safe area, I was not an evacuee. There were no air-raid shelters in our school at this time and so I ended my schooldays having lessons in my own, and other pupils' homes. We had alternate weeks of mornings or afternoons, in groups of about twenty children. We had no books or written work to do and lessons consisted mainly of a kind of lecture, followed by questions and answers. We had a canary in our house which insisted on being part of the general noise that we all made; our teacher could not make himself heard above the din. Poor Joey always ended up in the bedroom with the cover over his cage, or on the backyard wall.

As it happened, Norris Green did have a couple of bombs dropped on it. Two houses were destroyed in one raid, and Broadway railway bridge had a very near miss when a landmine left a huge crater nearby. Just a short distance further on, at Clubmoor, a train loaded with ammunition was hit. The terrific explosions, as sparks jumped from wagon to wagon, kept all of us in the surrounding area, dashing in and out of our shelters for most of the following day. Our windows all cracked, and the knocker on the front door rattled and banged with each explosion. The whole area was covered in white cotton waste from the packing on the ammunition. It made a bizarre sight, raining down on the area like snow.

I finally left school at Easter, 1940, and started work at Margaret Countess of Mayo, a very smart, fashionable shop in Bold Street. There actually was such a person as the Countess of Mayo, whom, I believe, allowed the use of her name for a fee. I suppose the name, and the coronet above it, lent the shop an air of exclusivity. The shop sold very expensive lingerie, blouses, knitwear, gloves and accessories. Initially, I was the general dog's body, vacuuming the floor and dusting the displays amongst other mundane jobs. Each morning I took the previous day's takings, in a blue cotton drawstring bag, to the Midlands Bank at the top of Bold Street. This was usually quite a large sum of money, but there were no fears about being mugged in those days. In fact, the word had a completely different meaning then; it was used when someone treated you to a night out, or bought you a drink, sweets, ice cream or a gift of some kind.

I also spent many hours in the freezing attic, ironing beautiful pure silk nightgowns and underwear for the window display, absolutely terrified in case I scorched anything. Sometimes I was so cold, I would warm the ironing pad with the iron and drape it round my shoulders for a few minutes. The iron was the only source of heat up there. It never entered my head to complain about it, but I don't think it would have made any difference, even if I had. There did not seem to be any laws about working conditions then.

It was not long before the air-raids started and most of the staff had already left to join the forces, or work on munitions. The window dresser and her family became evacuees and disappeared off to the safety of the Welsh hills. I had spent some time helping her with the displays, so when she left, I was promoted to window dresser. The only drawback was that I still had to fit in the ironing, and with the staff now reduced to five, I also had to serve customers.

With my promotion, my wage had risen from ten shillings per week, to twelve shillings and sixpence. We also earned commission of three pence in the pound on sales. However, there was a strict pecking order when it came to serving customers. First sales, a senior, went first, so naturally she always earned the most commission. Second or third, as the case may be, would only

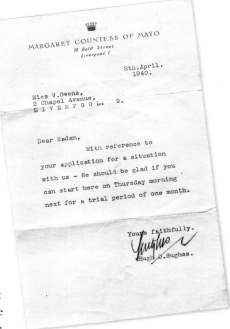

After leaving school, Vera secured herself a job in the exclusive, Countess of Mayo shop in Bold Street.

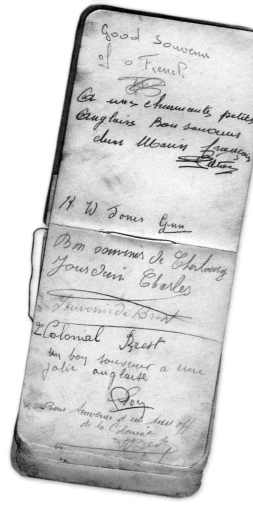

Vera has an autograph book full of similar messages to the ones above from French sailors who visited Liverpool during the war.

be called if there were customers waiting. When you were needed you were called, "Forward, Miss Owens", or whoever was next in line. Having the window and the displays and the ironing to attend to, I had little opportunity to earn much commission and so I asked for a rise. I was rewarded with an extra half-crown (two shillings and sixpence). I did find the temerity, some time later, to ask for more, and my pay was increased then to seventeen shillings and sixpence.

Many of our customers were in the services. Young men in their smart uniforms came into the shop to buy glamorous 'undies' for their wives or girlfriends. Some were very embarrassed and flustered when we asked what size bust the young lady had. While others, the sophisticated, man-about-town type, would sometimes embarrass us young girls with their personal comments, more so when there were two or three of them together. Not that they said anything really awful, it was just that we were shy and could not control our blushes. The girls of today would probably enjoy all the banter and give as good as they got.

As the months passed by, our stock of exclusive and beautiful things diminished. Quite a large proportion of our products came from the continent and so, after Dunkirk, in June 1940, there was no way it could be replaced. Luxury goods were off the market completely; everything was utility. We did get our quota of pure silk, fully-fashioned stockings and I don't know how, but people seemed to sense when a shop had some scarce little luxury for sale. A queue would form almost immediately the door opened. These sheer stockings, with a lovely dark seam and narrow dark panel, which came to a point an inch or two above the back of your shoe, were treasured. If you were lucky enough to obtain a pair of these stockings, they were kept carefully for very special occasions.

All stockings had a seam up the back in those days and the darker it was the better. To emphasise the seam, we wore our stocking inside out. If they were not fully fashioned, in other words, the shape knitted into the stocking, the heel area at the back of the ankle would have an unsightly fringe around it on the inside, which we carefully trimmed off. (Stockings ruined, and coupons wasted, if you nicked them with the scissors). A nice straight seam drew attention to your legs, and made them look shapely. Even when we used leg make-up, we drew a seam up the back. My mother always said it was very 'low', (not ladylike), to go about with bare legs; but we had no option during the war.

I had never met, or spoken to anyone from another land before the war began. My first encounter was just after the fall of France. I was staying with my grandmother in Aintree, which I often did. It was a Sunday morning and gran had opened her front door to bring in the milk from the step, when she was surprised to find three French sailors sitting there. They looked quite cute in their uniforms, which were very similar to our own, but they had red pompoms on their hats. They had been at sea when France capitulated, and had since received orders to return to the UK, rather than return to their home port and Hitler's clutches.

They spoke to gran, but she hadn't got a clue what they were saying. Using gestures, my uncle invited them in, and while gran was getting some

breakfast ready, he did his best to communicate with these young French boys. 'Parlez-vous', was about the limit of his French vocabulary, but not to be deterred, he tried to make them understand, every other word he said ending with an 'o'. He pointed to various objects around the house, did some mime play and generally waved his arms about. He looked and sounded so funny. The French boys could not speak English either but, mesmerised by my uncle, they sat there, hunching their shoulders and lifting their hands in the expressive way the continentals have. They pursed their lips, and repeated 'merci' over and over. Actually, we all got along quite well and managed in the end, to understand each other.

We saw a lot of our new friends in the short time they were stationed in Aintree and I still have my autograph book, which they, and their friends signed for me. I am ashamed to admit that I have never learnt another language and still cannot understand what they wrote in my book.

The American GIs eventually took over Aintree and Burtonwood, and they too were regular customers at Mayo's. Many of them married local girls, and when the war ended the GI brides sailed out to a new life in the USA. One of my friends went to live in Dallas, and has had a very happy life there ever since. Another found herself in the backwoods, in a hillbilly commune, made up of her husband's relations. Back home with his folks, he underwent a complete change of personality, unfortunately for the worse. It was not long before she came home again – alone.

The Countess of Mayo shop was very badly damaged in the May Blitz 1941. I walked all the way to work the next morning. We always went to work as usual after the raids, sometimes to find, as I did that morning, that it had been bombed or badly damaged in the raid. Everyone was so dazed and tired after long nights in the shelters. Our house was still intact, but we could tell by the red glow in the sky that the city had been very badly hit. I remember having to pick my way through bombed and battered streets and

Vera's mother used to sell National Savings stamps and she was awarded this medal in recognition of five years' service.

a succession of terrifying sights; the wardens and auxiliaries searching and shouting amongst the heaps of stones and girders for casualties; mothers with young children, dazed and bewildered and filthy with dust and soot, waiting to be taken to the rescue centre. There were no trams or buses running, no gas or electricity, and no water supplies. Most of the roads were impassable with bomb craters and vast piles of rubble, or roped off because of unexploded bombs. It was a scene of utter devastation and chaos.

The whole town seemed to be on fire. Lewis's and Blacklers were like huge furnaces. Our staff, and those from other Bold Street shops, were standing in Newington, which runs from Renshaw Street to Bold Street. We could go no further. Nearly all of the city centre was cordoned off. Firemen were still valiantly trying to stop the flames and the contents of the shops were strewn everywhere, all mangled and filthy amongst the rubble. Our boss was pleading with the wardens to let him through to the shop, but to no avail. All we could do was make our way home again, out of the fire-fighters' and wardens' way. I returned each morning and eventually we were allowed through to the shop. Nothing was salvageable; all the stock was soaking wet and filthy. For months afterwards a heavy pall of smoke hung over the city and a horrible dank smell of sodden burnt wood lingered for months.

On the bomb sites and other spare land in and around the city, emergency water supply tanks had been erected. These were of great help to the fire services during the air-raids. There were also barrage balloon sites and searchlights in the parks and on any other available land, manned by the men and women of the Armed Forces. Needless to say, these places attracted all the local kids, but they were never allowed to hang around for long.

Everyone did what they could to support the war effort. My mother went round the neighbours each week selling saving stamps and was given a medal commemorating five years' service. Some people collected paper and other salvage. Vegetable peelings and scraps of waste food were collected for pigswill, or to feed the hens. When I worked in the factory, we gave up our sweet ration and collected packets of cigarettes, books and magazines. We adopted a ward in Broadgreen Hospital, and each week two of the girls would visit the wounded and give them our small gifts. It was a very sad and shocking experience, coming face to face with all the wounded and maimed young men helplessly lying there.

Once you turned sixteen, your name was put on your street's fire watch rota, unless, of course, you were unable to do such a task. We used to go to St Teresa's schoolyard every Sunday morning to practise. An air-raid shelter would be filled with smoke, and two of us would have to crawl through on our hands and knees carrying a bucket of water and a stirrup pump. At the other end would be a fire, and we would have to put it out. I was quite small and slight in those days and I did not have the strength to get the pump working properly, so I would be given a bucket of sand and a shovel to douse the fire. I never did actually deal with an incendiary bomb myself, because during the air-raids, my stepfather would not let me out of the shelter. He was an air-raid warden, and patrolled the street during all the raids, making sure that there was not a speck of light showing anywhere. I must admit that I was not very keen to go. Thankfully, there were many civilians who were much braver than I was, they did many heroic things during that time with no recognition whatsoever for their valour. And no counselling for post-traumatic stress disorder either!

I was caught in an air-raid one evening on my way home from work on a tram. All the passengers had to hurry off the tram into a nearby shelter. The noise outside was terrific. Every so often you could hear the long whooshing whistle of a bomb hurtling down. A child started to cry and someone told him that if you could hear the whistle, there was no danger, because it was travelling overhead and would explode some distance away. That helped me to have courage too.

Eventually it quietened down and the warden let us out of the shelter into the blackout. The tramcar had gone. I still do not know whether it was blown to bits, or if it had moved to the depot, which was not very far away. There were shards of glass and piles of bricks underfoot, but we could not see them, it was much too dark, but we stumbled through them with every step we took. It was almost 11pm when I eventually reached home, after two more stops in different shelters on the way. I was only sixteen, and was absolutely petrified walking through the blackout on my own in the few quiet spells between the raids; the searchlights probing the sky and the barrage balloons standing out like ghostly blobs as the beams of light briefly caught them.

During the war, and for a period afterwards, everything had a utility label, from furniture to clothes. Coupons were issued to each family and these had to be produced before making any purchase.

Bold Street did get back on its feet again after a while. But it has never returned to its former glory, even now. It was such an elegant street, with many beautiful shops. I remember the big store, Cripps, another very expensive shop, and my favourite, Troxlers, the Swiss café, which sold the most delicious cakes. This famous street now looks so dirty and run down in comparison.

The shops were eventually patched up and made as sound as possible, but many of the businesses had packed up and gone. Blacklers split its various departments amongst these empty shops in Bold Street, until its own store could be rebuilt. With this new and different type of trade in Bold Street, we often had a Blacklers customer coming into Mayo's by mistake and asking, for instance, "wer's de 'ats girl?" Our manageress, who had a very superior air about her, would disdainfully direct these ladies to one of the Blacklers shops.

Most women went to a great deal of trouble to look smart, no matter what, and in fact this was strongly encouraged by the Government. It was thought to be a great morale booster for both sexes. We painstakingly copied the film stars' hairstyles; the sultry Veronica Lake look, or Rita Heyworth's bouncy style. We fashioned our hair into 'wind sweeps' with the help of a clothes peg. Or we might have had a ''V' for Victory roll', shaped at the back of the head. We queued for hours for a lipstick, or a box of powder, or maybe a comb and hairclips. The shortages made us more inventive and we trimmed

POST OFFICE TELEGRAM

PRIORITY-CC-THOMAS ARCHER 20 TEYNHAM CRESCENT LIVERPOOL 11 LANCS

DEEPLY REGRET TO INFORM YOU THAT YOUR SON WILLIAM JOHN ARCHER STOKER LT/KX-143051 HAS BEEN KILLED ON WAR SERVICE LETTER FOLLOWS - PATROLS LOWESTOFT +

During the war, everyone who had a son, husband or father who was away fighting, used to dread the sight of the telegraph boy coming down the road. One Sunday, in January 1944, the telegraph boy arrived at Vera's house and delivered this telegram bearing terrible news.

and re-trimmed what few clothes we had, to smarten them up and make them look different. We made earrings out of buttons and fuse wire and necklaces with shells that we painted and strung on coloured cord. We made belts with cellophane paper folded into strips and the pieces woven together and we used pipe cleaners for curlers or pieces of electric flex.

Our skirts were knee length, with three pleats in front and one at the back, so as not to waste material. Everything we bought had a utility label: clothes, bedding and furniture. Wooden-soled shoes became fashionable. Some of these had a leather hinge in the sole for easier walking. They looked quite smart and were very comfortable to wear. Leg make-up eked out the clothing coupons. It was lovely when the weather was fine, but what a mess when it rained, it ran in streaks down your legs. Leg make-up was the bane of my mother's life. I came home so many times too tired to wash it off and ended up with the sheets all streaked with 'tan'. When I went out in the evening, I was always given the same warnings:

"Don't you go too far from home," "Be in here by ten at the latest," and, "Make sure you wash that awful stuff off your legs before you get into bed."

The war changed all our lives completely from the start; things were never the same again. Quite early in the war my eldest stepsister married and left home to live with her in-laws, as her husband was on active service in the Army. Shortly after that, my eldest stepbrother, much to his distress, was found to be unfit to join the fighting forces. He went instead to Birmingham, to work in a munitions factory. Before long he was writing home, bragging about the good money he was earning and encouraging his younger brother to join him there. Billy had worked in the local Co-op store since he had left school, on a very low wage. He needed little encouragement and was off to Birmingham like a shot. He stayed there until he was called up and then joined the Royal Navy.

There was always an awful sense of dread at the sight of the telegraph boy going to someone's house. He came to ours one Sunday evening in January 1944. We all held our breath. Billy, had been killed in action in the English Channel, 'E boat alley', they called it. He would have been twenty-one in the July of that year. His convoy had been torpedoed with the loss of five ships and a great loss of life. We were all shocked and stunned into inaction by this news. My stepfather was the first to move, without saying a word he went upstairs to hide his grief. He would not allow any of us near him for quite a while. We felt an awful sense of helplessness, which added to our grief and sorrow. A policeman arrived later in the evening, with a letter authorising a travel warrant for my parents.

My stepfather and mother went down to Penzance, where a mass funeral and service had been arranged. Whilst this was taking place, the Germans were shelling the English coast from across the Channel, and everyone was issued with a tin hat.

We were all devastated at the loss of Bill, and I could not believe that he had been killed. For a long time afterwards I felt convinced that he would come home again, even after the war had ended.

In the following three weeks, three more young men from our road also lost their lives; all of them were under twenty-one years of age. It was a terribly sad and depressing time. Looking back I do not know how our parents coped with it all. They really were stoical and brave.

It was February and the weather was very cold and there was a shortage of coal. We had a gas fire in the bedroom but it was inconvenient and expensive to have on during the day. My mother used to mix something with water, I think it was washing soda, which she poured over the coal dust and slack. This made it gel together and it would burn for longer. Every morning mother raked out every cinder and used them to start the fire, and once it got going, it was backed up with the slack solution and other household rubbish such as tea-leaves. None of us dared to poke that fire, it was left to smoulder all day, no leaping flames up the chimney. But it kept the water warm and the coal lasted longer.

The beginning of 1944 was a grim time for everyone. Every single commodity was in short supply. If you saw a queue you joined it, regardless of what was on offer. If it was not to your liking, someone else would be glad of it. On my way home from the night shift one morning I joined a queue outside Coopers in Church Street. I stood there for an hour and came away triumphant, clutching a set of pans for my bottom draw. On another occasion I was lucky and bought a hearthrug from TJ Hughes in London Road. It was the custom then to collect things for your future home (your bottom draw). The pans and mat were all I was able to put in mine.

My boyfriend and I were planning to get married around this time. He was due for some leave from the Navy around June. Family and friends were very kind, contributing whatever food coupons they could spare for my wedding cake ingredients, such as sugar and dried fruit. The cake was eventually ready, and a friend had made my dress, all we needed now was the bridegroom. June arrived and there was no sign of him, no letters even. The days passed and still no sign. Then the news broke that our troops had invaded France. It was 'D Day', which explained Pat's absence. He was in the Royal Navy, but based on the merchant ships as a gunner, the DEMS (Defensively Equipped Merchant Ships). All mail from serving men and women had been cancelled during this time for security reasons.

I discovered, a long time afterwards, that on D Day, and in later weeks, he was in the midst of the invasion, on a ship loaded with ammunition supplies for the troops. He arrived home for Christmas at the end of the year, and we got married on his 21st Birthday on the 30 December 1944. I was nineteen. All of our friends were overseas, so a casual acquaintance was our best man. We had two cars, one from each of two different companies. No photographer, we made do with a couple of snaps that a friend of a friend

This gravestone, in a military cemetery in Penzance, belongs to Vera's stepbrother, Bill Archer, who was killed in action in 1944 in the English Channel, or 'E-boat alley' as it was called.

Vera remembers queueing outside Coopers for hours and eventually emerging triumphant, clutching a set of pans for her bottom drawer.

took of us five days later. My bouquet was somewhat the worse for wear by then, but the photograph is a precious keepsake of our wartime wedding. Pat returned to his ship, and I did not see him again until after the war had come to an end with victory in Japan. He was in Canada on VE day.

When my turn came for call up at the age of eighteen, I was given the choice of the NAAFI, public transport, or war work. I chose the latter, I just could not imagine myself putting some burly dockers off the overcrowded last tram. I was sent to the training centre in Stopgate Lane for twelve weeks. We were taught how to read a blueprint, set up a machine, grind tools and read a micrometer. I was engaged then and planning to be married, so this gave me compassionate grounds to stay in Liverpool. Other single girls were sent to factories in the Midlands, or Manchester. After training I was sent to the Automatic Telephone Company, in Edge Lane. We did twelve hour shifts, a fortnight about of days and nights. How well I remember struggling to keep my eyes open in the small hours of the morning, to the sound of the 'Ink Spots' singing *This is a lovely way, to spend an evening*. When the war ended we were told that we had been making 'George', the automatic pilot, which had guided many wounded pilots safely home to base.

After working in a nice genteel shop, the factory was a dramatic change for me. The noise of the machines, the pulleys and the belts, constantly whirling round, frightened me at first. We wore boiler suits and a mesh hat with a hard peek at the front. Every wisp of hair had to be tucked into it. There were one or two girls who ignored these instructions, and they had very nasty and painful accidents, such as a piece being torn out of their scalp. We had to remove rings and other jewellery in case they caught in the machinery, as you could lose a finger or hand if they did. I soon got used to factory life and made some very good friends, who took me under their wing, so to speak, and protected me from the jokers. Newcomers had all kinds of tricks played on them, such as being sent to the stores for a 'long stand'.

On the night shift we were allowed one late pass a fortnight. One girl returned to the factory, after her night out, a bit the worse for drink. The guard at the gate would not let her in and she was fined, and warned that it would be prison the next time it happened.

We were made to understand that we were on active service, every bit as much as someone who was in the Armed Forces. While I was still training we were asked to join the various parades in town. Experienced people could not be spared from their jobs for this. For instance there would be 'Battleship Week', 'Spitfire Week', or 'Tank Week'. We would assemble in town and march through the streets in our boiler suits, along with the ARP (Air Raid Precaution) wardens and other auxiliaries. There would be various local bands with us and the crowds watching waved their Union Jacks, clapping and shouting three cheers for the war workers as we passed by. We loved the support, the factory workers did not seem to be appreciated as much as the servicemen and women. But, it was all very patriotic and rousing, which, after all, was the motive behind it.

There was a wonderful camaraderie among the people during the war, everyone was willing to share what they had, and help wherever they could.

The Government realised the importance of keeping up the morale of the people when times were bleak and depressing and so, as much entertainment as possible was provided everywhere. There were the radio programmes, *Workers' Playtime* and *Music While You Work*, in the factories. Concert parties, musicians and actors entertained us at lunchtime, not only in the canteens but also in the libraries, art galleries and concert halls around the city.

We danced at the Grafton, music provided by Mrs Wilf Hamer, and her wonderful girls' band. Other popular dance halls were the Rialto, Reeces, and the Tower Ballroom in New Brighton. Locally, we had Swainsons in Walton Hall Avenue, and Barlows Lane and the Aintree Institute. Every local church hall had a Saturday night dance and all of them had a live band. The American servicemen made a big impact on the local girls but there were men from other countries too; new faces every week as the forces moved on. We enjoyed ourselves at every available opportunity. Someone coming home on leave was always an excuse for a 'do'. There were no lavish buffets, just a small keg of beer for the men and a shandy, or maybe, a port and lemonade for the girls.

We carried on living the best we could amidst all the tragedy and mayhem around us. Thousands lost their lives or were maimed when the bombing started and there were many unsung heroes and heroines among the ordinary people at that time. So many lost their homes and everything they possessed. My husband's family had twenty extra people, three of them pregnant, sharing their home at one time, all of them relations who had been bombed out. One of the expectant mothers was taken to hospital during the May Blitz. The ambulance had to stop and change its route so often during the journey, that she thought she was never going to survive the ordeal.

I am left with a great admiration for the women, especially mothers, many of whom were left alone to cope with all the problems that the war brought them. Coping first of all with the evacuation scheme, which was surely a wrench to say the least. Then there was rationing and shortages of necessities and having to provide nourishing and appetising meals for hungry children. It was the women who had to calm their children's fears during the air-raids, who had to deal with the trauma of being bombed out, and losing all their prized possessions. And of course they had to live with the ever-constant anxieties for absent husbands and loved ones on active service.

One particularly lovely memory I have of those wartime years is of the sky at night. The clear moonlit nights were as bright as day, so beautiful, but sadly, these were the nights we dreaded most during the air-raids. There were also the dark velvet nights too, when the stars looked so big and so near that you felt as though you could just reach out and touch them. I still look up at the stars, but the bright city lights dim all their true beauty now.

It was all such a long time ago and the world is so different now. But if I want to evoke my memories of those wartime days, I only have to listen to a recording of the big band sound of Glenn Miller, Benny Goodman, or Tommy Dorsy, and I am back in the Tower Ballroom, dancing the night away, without a care in the world. The good times had a very special quality in those wartime years and remembering them always leaves me with a feeling of nostalgia.

Dorothy Curl – Born 1926

I was born in 1926, the fourth child in a family of ten children – seven girls and three boys. I was born at Number 1 Arrow Street, in the district of Edge Hill, about a mile from Liverpool city centre. It was a one way street leading from Wavertree Road. All the trams and buses travelled along this road to the suburbs like Childwall and Woolton, which made it a very busy main road.

A child could have four rides for a penny on the tramcars in those days and during the school holidays we took full advantage of this. We often went off in a group to the parks and woods with a bottle of lemonade, made with lemonade powder, and a packet of sandwiches, coming home tired and hungry after a wonderful day out.

At the top of Arrow Street was a brick wall about ten feet high, on the other side of which was Edge Hill goods station, with wagons constantly clanking up and down the tracks. The noise that they made was a constant nuisance to the residents but there was no procedure for complaints in those days. Children playing in the street were often heard singing:

> *Piggy on the railway, picking up stones.*
> *Along came an engine and broke Piggy's bones.*
> *"Oh," said Piggy, "that's not fair."*
> *"Well," said the engine, "I don't care."*

Perhaps the purpose of the rhyme was to remind children of the dangers that lay beyond the wall. I certainly never heard of any child having an accident on the railway. We did go round to the goods yard on occasions to retrieve a ball, but we would always look for a man to help us. On the whole, children were well disciplined both in the home and at school, and would probably take notice when danger was pointed out to them.

The street consisted of a variety of terraced houses, about twenty altogether, four of which had front gardens. These houses were at the top end of the street away from the main road and there was an entry at the rear of the houses that separated them from the railway goods station. The house opposite ours had a stable attached where a horse and cart were kept. The family that lived there was financially much better off than ours. I remember

Dorothy was evacuated to Wales during the early part of the war and was billeted, along with two of her sisters, with foster parents, 'Auntie' Blodwen and 'Uncle' Tom. Unlike many evacuees, her time with them was a happy one.

the young woman from that house going on holiday to Mold, in North Wales, an unusual event in those days. She sent a picture postcard to my mother, who must have treasured it, as I still have it to this day.

My parents started their married life in 1919, and their first-born child was a girl, born in 1920. She was given my mother's Christian name, Pamela. By 1935 there were eight children. Our house in Arrow Street was a terrace with a front parlour. There was also a kitchen, or dining room, and also a back kitchen with a cold water tap, a sink and a very old gas cooker. The lavatory was down the backyard and upstairs there were three bedrooms.

My grandmother, or 'nin' as we called her, grandad and an aunt, all shared the house with us, or rather, we shared it with them. We lived in the parlour where my mother and father also slept, and all of the children shared the front bedroom, which was the largest room in the house. The only lighting was from a gas mantle, and we used a candle to light us up to bed. My mother heated water on the fire and she kept a bucket of water in the cupboard. The old gas cooker in the kitchen was my nin's, and we shared it with her.

This cramped lifestyle continued until about 1935 when my mother, father and eight children moved to a terraced house in the next street. A whole house to ourselves: Number 12 Ash Street. The accommodation was identical to my nin's. But the new house was in a dreadful condition, infested with bugs and cockroaches. It had to be scrubbed from top to bottom.

My mother went on to have her ninth child in 1937. We had an exceptionally good landlord who seemed to be a bit of a philanthropist, he was so devoted to improving conditions for his tenants. Firstly, electricity was installed in the downstairs rooms. This cost us an extra shilling on the rent. Next came the removal of the large black range in the kitchen, which was replaced by a beautiful green and cream tiled fireplace, complete with a back boiler to heat the water. A bath and sink were also installed in the small bedroom with again, a little more to pay on the rent of the house.

Having a bathroom was all very well, but it meant the loss of a much-needed bedroom for such a large family. However, nin and grandad came to the rescue, and it was arranged that two of the boys would sleep in their house. So, each evening off they went down the back entry to Arrow Street and to bed, returning home for breakfast the next morning.

In the 1930s my mum used 'Lively Polly' washing powder and inside each packet was a coupon which could be saved and used to send away for gifts. I remember cutting out coupon after coupon until we had amassed about four hundred. Few people in our neighbourhood were lucky enough to own a camera but my Mum had always longed to have one and she 'bought' one with the coupons. Throughout the war she used the camera to take pictures of the family, so I am lucky to have a visual record of my childhood and of all my brothers and sisters.

Life in the 1930s was never to be the same again for our family. The 3 September 1939 is a date fixed forever in my memory. It was the day the Prime Minister of Great Britain made the announcement that this country was now at war with Germany. Great disruption came with the start of the Second World War. Five of the children in my family were evacuated to North Wales and soon afterwards, in 1940, my mother had her tenth child.

This would be a war that would reach out beyond the battlefields to involve the lives of women and children, because of the intervention of the aeroplane. The government of the day had already prepared a vast evacuation scheme, which would move children from the inner cities to the safety of the countryside, and it was put into operation immediately the war began.

We lived about a mile from the city centre in an area close to many of the targets which the enemy would seek out to destroy: the docks, shipping, railways and factories. Five of our family of nine children were of school age and so eligible to be part of this mass evacuation of children from Liverpool.

Along with three sisters and a brother, I was taken on a very long journey from Edge Hill railway station, which was within sight of our home. Mother had provided us with a pillowcase each, containing a change of clothes and a few other belongings. Off we went with our gas masks slung over our shoulders, a few sandwiches and tears in our eyes.

To our dismay, we were separated at an early stage of the journey. Edith, who was five, was taken with the infant department of our school. John, who was ten, was taken with the boys – girls and boys were separated in those days at junior level. The other three girls, including myself, stayed together. The journey seemed never-ending and we had not been given any information as to where we were being taken. Finally, late on Sunday evening, we arrived in a village called Llanberis, at the bottom of a steep pass, several miles from Caernarfon in North Wales.

It appeared that all the children from our school, Clint Road, Edge Hill, had been taken to the surrounding villages to be billeted. The school hall was crammed with people with unfamiliar faces milling around. I remember feeling utterly devastated, lost and lonely. Then we learned with alarm that there was no available billet for three children; we were to be separated. That is, until a dear lady, obviously noticing our distress, agreed to take all three of us into her home. This was to be a happy time for us, but at first we longed to find Edith and John.

All evacuees were issued with a postcard on which to write their new address, to be returned home as soon a possible. Soon after our arrival my mother sent us Edith's address. She was about three miles away from us, and our brother John was sixteen miles away. We found out much later that he was having a very unhappy time – his temporary foster parents were unkind and gave him little food. When our parents eventually visited and realised the situation, they applied to have him moved to the same village as Edith. He was then billeted on a farm where he was expected to work very hard; up at 5.30, milking the cows, followed by many other unpleasant tasks on the farm. He remembers many a morning falling asleep whilst milking the cows and toppling off his milking stool.

Not only were we far away from our city home, this was actually another country, with its own strange, sing-song language that we had never heard before and couldn't understand. But we had our school friends around us and this helped to keep the tears away. The mountain scenery around Llanberis was breath-takingly beautiful and we spent many hours exploring the countryside. School was attended on a part-time basis only, sharing the classrooms with the Welsh children, so we had plenty of leisure time. We

Unlike many ordinary people at the time, Dorothy's mother had a small camera and so Dorothy has a good pictorial record of her childhood.

Opposite: Dorothy's mother, father and older sister (note the brick air-rad shelter behind her mother).

Above: foster parents 'Auntie' Blodwen and 'Uncle' Tom and Dorothy and two of her sisters in Wales during the evacuation.

Dorothy's mother brought her new baby and Dorothy's younger brother, Eric, out to North Wales to visit her other children. They are pictured here at the waterfall at Llanberis.

Dorothy's elder sister Margaret with her future husband in front of the family house. Note the windows criss-crossed with tape to prevent flying glass in the event of an air-raid.

settled down well with an occasional visit to see Edith and John. Our foster parents, whom we referred to as Auntie Blodwen and Uncle Tom, were very kind and thoughtful people.

Within a few weeks, some of our friends returned home to their families. The air-raids which had been expected did not happen. So we remained in Wales with a feeling of desertion by our own family and increasingly heavy hearts, even though my mother wrote regularly and sent us pocket money. It was usually a one-shilling postal order that we cashed at the post office in the village. Edith remembers her friend, Norma, telling her that she was going back to Liverpool. She had cried bitterly and felt very lonely and abandoned when she had gone. Tragically, in November 1940, Norma and her family were killed when a bomb exploded on a building in Edge Hill, where they had sought shelter from an air-raid.

As Christmas approached, and most of our friends had already gone back home, it was obvious that we were to remain in our new home. Mother continued to write, saying she was saving up to come and visit us. We transferred to the school in the next village, which was to be a new experience, travelling on the bus each day. We were such a mixed age group in that class that I am afraid we were just occupied rather than taught.

We attended the Welsh Chapel on Sundays with Auntie Blodwen and Uncle Tom. There was a great deal of singing, and our contribution of reciting a verse from the Bible in the Welsh language was no hardship for us, as we attended Sunday School and church back home, but we missed listening to our own language.

The months dragged on and we received news from home of the birth of a new baby sister on the 23 April 1940, my mother's tenth child. Mother, father, little brother and new baby finally came to visit us in the late summer of 1940; a very happy occasion, as one would expect. I accompanied them back to Liverpool, with very little confidence, to earn my own living. Leaving my sisters behind was a terrible wrench which brought much heartache.

We stayed in touch with Auntie Blodwen and Uncle Tom until 1984, when Blodwen died. We spent many happy holidays with them over the years and they were delighted with our own children.

I personally never felt unloved by my parents; in all good faith they felt their decision to send us away was the best they could do in the circumstances which faced them at the time. But I am afraid that life was never to be the same again in the Liverpool household, as we inevitably grew apart during our separation. Life in the country had been a totally different experience for us evacuees, and inevitably coloured our view of the world from then on.

Once back at home my social life once more revolved around our local church, St Catherine's, Tunnel Road. Amongst the many activities offered by the Girls' Guildery at the church, were embroidery sessions and PT lessons using dumbells – the latter usually rousingly accompanied by the piano. Every Saturday, rambles were organised by the club, usually on the Wirral, and we would all go over together on the ferry. The Guidery was a poor person's Girl Guides. It was recognised that to buy a uniform was beyond the

Dorothy's social life, like many teenagers at the time, revolved around Sunday School. Here, with two friends, she is selling flags for 'waifs and strays'.

means of poor families, so we just had to wear a white blouse with a bow and a hat. My two elder sisters eventually became leaders at the Guidery.

I was also a member of the Young People's Union where we used to sew things to raise money for the missionaries and for one week each year we would sell flags for the 'waifs and strays' – we were not very politically correct in those days! My mum always saw to it that we all attended church and Sunday School - it was the focus of our lives, and the Sunday School outing was one of the highlights of our year.

The reason I had come back from evacuation was, of course, because I was now of working age. I started working as an apprentice tailor at Wetherall's workshop in Parr Street – the firm also had a shop in Bold Street. After twelve months I realised that I could make far more money working at Bear Brand in Woolton, making silk stockings, and I was taken on as a machinist. This also meant that I was able to wear fully-fashioned stockings throughout the war, a rare luxury, as we were allowed a number of pairs each year. After the war, Bear Brand moved into the city and I became a charge-hand tutor.

Soon after I returned home, I had to come to terms with another family tragedy; the busy Wavertree Road, which led into the city, and which we had all survived as children, eventually claimed the life of my parents' ninth child, Eric. I was often put in charge of looking after my little brother Eric, but one evening I was out on a ramble with the church club and my dad was listening to the six o'clock news on the radio. Eric was playing in the lobby, when he somehow managed to climb over the special wooden gate which dad had made to stop him from running out into the road. My grandfather saw him

Sister Irene with wooden scooter and little brother Eric who was tragically killed by a bus just after his fourth birthday, after surviving the Liverpool Blitz.

Dorothy with her favourite doll, a prize from Sunday School, awarded for presenting a bouquet to a VIP.

Sister Edith with her friend Norma on evacuation in North Wales. Norma returned to Liverpool and was killed, with eight members of her family in the Durning Road tragedy.

at the bottom of our street and told him to go back home. But instead he ran into Wavertree Road, probably trying to get to the sand in the bombed out shops across the road. After living through the dreadful eight-day May Blitz and emerging unharmed, Eric was tragically killed on the road by a bus at the age of four years and nine days. I remember my mum wearing black for months afterwards and she coped with her grief by reading book after book.

At the start of the air-raids in 1940, we initially used a large underground shelter in Wavertree Park but then we heard about a college in Durning Road where preparation had been made in the cellars for people to shelter from air-raids. People had started to take the war very seriously by this time and thought it best to use this shelter, there being no room in the backyards of their terraced houses for an Anderson shelter. There was a large brick shelter in our street, but the Durning Road shelter was comfortable and warm and people preferred it to the brick shelters which were cold and damp.

Once we had suffered a few air-raids we didn't wait for the sirens to go off, but would set off every evening armed with blankets and food for Durning Road and settle down for the night. Although the shelter was comfortable and warm because of the large boilers which were down there, it was also very noisy, and Irene, my six-month-old baby sister, would cry all night. So my mum decided instead to use the large communal brick shelter which had been built in our street, but only when the sirens went off, as it was too uncomfortable to stay there all night.

The first night that we stayed at home my dad, who was an ARP warden, happened to call in. When he found us all sitting in the house he was absolutely furious with mum for putting us at risk and he made his feelings known - the air was blue!

However, about two weeks later, the Durning Road shelter received a direct hit in what Churchill described as one of the worst civilian tragedies of the war up to that time. In order not to damage morale, the newspapers at the time were only allowed to report that there had been 'a large loss of life' and were forbidden from giving details of the tragedy in which upwards of 170 people were killed. Some of the victims were killed outright, but many others were scalded with steam escaping from exploding boilers, or burnt when gas escaping from broken pipes burst into flames.

We knew many of the people who were killed and realised only too well that we could so easily have been amongst them. Our neighbour two doors down lost her two daughters and their husbands, as well as her grandchildren Jean, Henry, Ethel, Sybil and Norma - my sister Edith's seven-year-old friend who had returned early from evacuation in Wales. One of her grandchildren, George, survived, although he was badly injured. Left an orphan, he was eventually shipped off to Australia, when his grandmother was unable to look after him any longer.

Somehow, we all managed to survive the war but it took its toll in many different ways. Pamela, my eldest sister, joined the ATS, rather than doing war work in a factory, but she contracted pneumonia and then TB which damaged her health to such an extent that she was unable to have children

This group of friends and neighbours including Dorothy's father (second right, front row) and mother second left, second row) off to Blackpool in 1938, includes many who were killed in November 1940 in the bombing of the college in Durning Road, Edge Hill.

of her own, although she did go on to marry and adopt two lovely children. Hilda, who was evacuated with me to Llanberis, was deeply upset by the wrench away from home, and after I came back to Liverpool she ran away several times, despite the kindness of Blodwen and Tom. My brother John was very unhappy during his stay in Wales, even after he had been moved. When asked why he had not written of his problems to my parents, he admitted that he could not read or write properly, although he went on to become a great reader. I seemed to survive relatively unscathed, and in 1948, I married my fiancé Douglas, who was in the artillery and took part in the D Day landings, and we are still together today.

In fact, although none of us stayed on at school beyond the age of fourteen, we all reached a good standard of education. My sister Sarah hated the factory work which she was expected to do and eventually trained to be a teacher. At the age of forty, with my three children growing up, I decided that it was about time that I went back to college and I trained to become a nursery nurse. With the benefit of better educational opportunities, my children, and those of my brothers and sisters, have set their sights higher and many of them have entered the professions.

Separated from his sisters, and mistreated by his foster parents in Wales, Dorothy's brother John was very unhappy and had to be moved. Next he found himself on a farm where he had to get up at five o'clock in the morning to milk the cows.

Dorothy married Douglas in 1948, surrounded by her pals from work.

Mollie Connor – Born 1926

I was born during 1926 into poverty and recession. Conditions then for the working class were very bad. There were no social services, and the housing conditions left much to be desired. We lived in a one-room house in a back court in Fulford Street in Kirkdale. (Kirkdale, incidentally, is named in the Doomsday Book). Our only water supply was from the single tap in the court, which we shared with other neighbours.

I was the eldest of seven children. My dad was a seaman. How my mam managed to stay sane I don't know, because at one stage she had five children in one room. But then most of the other families in the street were in the same situation. Most couples had large families, as there was no birth control in those days.

I went to Our Lady Immaculate School in York Terrace at the time of the Elementary Education System, with very large classes of at least thirty children and the emphasis on the rote method of learning. Although I can understand why this method has fallen out of favour, it did not do me any harm. I can still recite all my tables and do mental arithmetic. The classes, from the juniors upwards, were called 'Standards'. Standard 1 was the equivalent of Year 3 (seven to eight-year-olds) continuing up to Standard 7, the top class of the seniors (thirteen to fourteen-year-olds).

Our street was off Great Homer Street, which started at Kirkdale Road and finished at Mile End. It was full of shops, pubs, churches and businesses and on every street corner there were women with handcarts selling fruit and vegetables. The street was always bustling and alive with people, and above the general clamour, came the cries of the handcart women selling their goods. At night the shops would be all lit up and not barricaded as they are today. Hordes of children played in the streets and we were never short of playmates. The street was our territory, it belonged to us and, because there were no cars, our mothers felt it was quite safe to let us play unsupervised.

My friends and I used to go looking in the shop windows, especially Reuben's, the shoe shop, admiring the shoes we could never have. The best we could hope for was a pair of pumps. We also looked longingly at the sweets in Hignett's window and the coats and suits in Charles the Tailors. In

This picture of a typical court illustrates what dark, dreary places they were. During her early years Molly lived in a single room in a back court in Kirkdale, with just a single tap for all the families.

later years, when I was about fifteen, the tailor made me a made-to-measure gabardine coat, paid for weekly. I can still remember to this day when I first wore that coat, with a pair of ankle band patent leather shoes and white socks. When I went to church on that Sunday, I walked down the aisle feeling like a princess; I thought I looked lovely.

Nearby was Bradley's, the factory that made overalls. All the factory workers used our street, (everyone walked to work then), to get to the factory. I used to love sitting on our steps watching them and listening to them laughing and talking. There was also Flanagan's the wireworks on Kirkdale Road, and in our street there was a builder's yard. All the workmen there used to whistle and shout after the girls on their way to and from work.

Even on a Sunday our street was very busy. Bullen's Dancing Academy was just across the road, where they used to hold afternoon tea dances. All the girls who went there used to wear long dresses and dancing shoes. I used to love watching them as they paraded past our house. I promised myself that when I grew up I too would go to Bullen's. I did eventually get there, but it was all changed by then. It was wartime, and austerity affected every area of or lives – so no tea dances and lovely dresses. It was the time of the Jive and Jitterbug, exciting new dances that were all the rage. The more sedate ballroom dancing was losing its popularity.

When Christmas time comes around nowadays, I always think back to my Christmases in the 1930s. There was no picking what presents you wanted, we received exactly the same thing every year. Our Winnie and I got a cardboard sweet shop, with little jars of sweets and a tin till with tin coins. Our Pat and Jimmy got a bugle with chocolates attached to it. Billie and Charlie were too young to know about presents, so they were just given sweets, an apple and a tangerine in their stockings.

But we did get to go to parties given by the church charities. There was Christmas breakfast on Christmas morning in the Methodist Church in Boundary Street, which we called the red brick church, for obvious reasons. A few weeks before Christmas we would start going to the services on a Sunday evening to get a ticket for the party. Mr Bell, the minister, knew that we were Catholics, and understood only too well why we came to the services, but he just welcomed us all. We enthusiastically joined in the unfamiliar hymns displayed on the big hymn sheets, my favourite being *All things bright and beautiful*.

On Christmas morning we would set off for the church, full of eager anticipation for the feast in store for us. Inside were long trestle tables, laden with meat pies, sausage rolls, sandwiches and drinks, and a jovial Father Christmas, who gave us all a present. When I think back to those days before the war, I realise how good those people were to give up their time and provide all those treats for us.

There were lots of very hungry people during the recession in the 1930s; the poverty suffered was extreme, not just in this country, but worldwide. Even in America people were dying of starvation. It has been argued that wars are a necessary evil; they boost the economy and provide jobs. I am inclined to believe that there is some truth in the argument, because during the Second World War, and all the years since, I can thankfully say that I have never experienced poverty like I did during my childhood in the thirties.

I was thirteen years old when the war started. My two brothers, a sister and myself were all evacuated. We went to stay in a village called Brosely, not far from the ironbridge in Shropshire. On the day of the evacuation we were instructed to assemble at our school. We had to take along our gas masks, name tags, our clothes in a brown paper bag (not much, just a change of underwear), a towel, flannel, a change of top clothes and a couple of jam butties for the journey. We were then taken to Lime Street Station, where we queued up to board our trains. Looking back, I can remember that I was filled with excitement. I had never been on a train, never even been outside of Liverpool. To me it was a huge adventure and I could not wait for the train to take us away to our new home.

Being an evacuee was the most memorable experience in my life and our time in Shropshire was like being in another world; no poverty, and living in a lovely home. I was so happy; it completely changed my outlook on life. You could say, I saw how the other half lived. I came to understand how naive I had been. I had always assumed that everyone's lifestyle was the same as my own, living in street communities and grinding poverty from which there was no escape.

I was billeted with my sister, and Lucy Caley, a classmate, with a Mr and Mrs Bickley. She was a music teacher and he worked at the aerodrome. They had no children of their own and they lived in a beautiful big house which had a large garden and an apple orchard. To me it was paradise. We went to school in the village hall, where dances were also held. Oh! what wonderful memories I have of village life. I went to my very first dance at the village hall with the rest of my school – absolute heaven!

Unfortunately this happy interlude as an evacuee did not last long, only about six months, as I had to return home to Liverpool to help my mother after she had had another baby. With my father away at sea, she was unable to care for the baby and my two baby brothers single-handedly. As I was now the eldest of seven children, I was summoned from my brief rural sojourn to help her.

I revisited Brosely years later, hoping to recapture some of the atmosphere of the place. It was a mistake. My beautiful old home had been turned into a launderette, the village hall into a supermarket and none of the old familiar places remained. But for me, that little Shropshire village will always be stored in my memory, as the place which opened my eyes to another world, full of wonderful possibilities.

I returned to Liverpool just in time for the air-raids which started in the last three months of 1940. The raids would start in the early evening and thunder on relentlessly until the early hours of the morning. As soon as the sirens whined out their awful warning, we dashed to the shelters in the cellars under the shops; most of our street went there too, and we all had our own places. The shelter was cold, noisy and cramped and it was very tiring having to uproot ourselves night after night. But we did feel safe being with friends and people we knew. There was a man who used to play the accordion and others had mouth organs. We all sang along with them to keep the children happy and lull them to sleep.

There were three main types of gas mask. This one, the Mickey Mouse gas mask, was red and blue and designed for young children up to the age of seven.

Gas masks were carried in boxes on string like a shoulder bag.

This is the standard gas mask which was issued to adults and children from seven upwards.

Young women used to decorate their gas mask boxes by making knitted or crocheted covers which co-ordinated with their outfits.

We lived not far from the docks, so our neighbourhood got quite a battering from the German bombers. It was also very stressful for my mam, being on her own with three young children with only me to help her. Occasionally, when the siren sounded and she was feeling particularly weary, instead of going to the shop cellars, she would decide to take the risk and stay at home. She huddled us all together and we would squeeze into the space under the stairs, where we listened to the incessant bombardment and felt the vibrations when a bomb fell close by. But then it happened. On the 20 December 1940 we were bombed out. We were lucky – that night our guardian angels were watching over us. The bomb fell on the house next door and completely demolished it. Our house got the blast. The roof was destroyed, and the bedrooms. Thankfully, the stairs held and although we were very badly shaken, we escaped unharmed. The air-raid wardens soon arrived and took us to St John's church hall, because what was left of our house was unsafe.

We never returned to our house. We spent that Christmas and New Year in different church halls: St Teresa's in Norris Green and then St Matthew's, Clubmoor. There were dozens of bombed-out families living under the same roof, sleeping on mattresses on the floor and fed by Meals-on-Wheels. We had scouse for our Christmas dinner that year. After a few weeks of camping out in the halls, we were allocated a house in Huyton. We lived there for two years, and because it was on the outskirts of Liverpool, we were safe from the air-raids.

At fourteen you left school and had to go out to work to bring in money to help the family. You handed your wages over to your mum and in my case I was given one shilling pocket money. You could not afford to go out on dates, or courting, until you were about seventeen or eighteen, when you earned more money and could afford to go to the cinema or a dance. Before that, the street was the meeting ground for lads and girls; playing games together, or meeting in the ice cream parlours on the street corners.

On Great Homer Street, before the war, there were lots of ice cream parlours. When the Italians joined the war with the Germans, all the ice cream shops were smashed up and destroyed by gangs. But local people joined together to save one particular shop; everybody liked Louie, the owner, he wouldn't hurt a fly. But, sadly, the shop was bombed when the street was hit in December 1940.

My first job was in a doll factory. I hated it and did not stay long. The war brought with it lots of jobs and I moved to a tin factory and then to Paton Calverts on Edge Lane. It was here that I learned the facts of life (or 'the birds and the bees' as they were euphemistically called). I was very naive and had only gleaned snippets here and there at school, at work, or from friends. I had refused to believe them; my mum and dad would definitely not do things like that! In the canteen I would listen to the married women and older girls talking, pretending, of course, that I knew it all. The information I gleaned may have been a bit sketchy, but it was all I had; my mother never told me anything, it just wasn't discussed.

Even though there was a war on, I enjoyed my teenage years. I was suddenly grown up and looked forward to nights spent dancing at the

Grafton with my workmates and drinking in the pubs in town when I was eighteen. Those times were really wonderful; jive and rock 'n' roll, and ballroom dancing on a Thursday night. 'Come Dancing' with Victor Sylvester. We met so many different nationalities; soldiers, sailors and airmen and everywhere there was that powerful feeling of togetherness. So many people of my generation agree that the war years were a time of mutual help and co-operation. It was like being in one big, happy family. These were my teenage years. There was certainly a large measure of tragedy, sorrow and tears, but there was also joy and many lovely memories to treasure.

There were shortages of many items, both luxury and basic. Nylons were in very short supply, unless you had a friend who went to sea. Instead, we used to wear leg-tan, which made your legs look lovely. My friends and I used to buy our leg-tan from Houghton's in Old Swan. It was their own make and a lovely, natural shade. So many of the others were awful. Make-up was also scarce but I started to wear it as soon as I could afford it. We did not wear much, just a bit of Snowfire or Ponds cream, and powder and lipstick. I had to remove every trace of it before I went home, because my dad would not let me or my sisters 'paint our faces' as he called it. I still use the same make-up today. I have never used mascara, in fact I don't even know how!

The day we were bombed out, 20 December, was also the day I met my husband-to-be, thrown together by momentous events beyond our control. We met in St Teresa's church hall; I was fourteen and so was he. We were neighbours on the mattresses on the floor.

Looking back now, the war marked the beginning of the end of a way of life.

MAKE-DO AND MEND says *Mrs. Sew-and-Sew*

YOUR

Save Coupons

YOUR MENDED CLOTHES *Mean* MORE BATTLE CLOTHES

MAKE-DO AND MEND

SAVE MATERIAL

Join A MAKE-DO & MEND CLASS

Dance Frock into Undies

IT WILL MAKE

a slip
a House
&panties

5½D

How to patch elbows and knees

Tina Silverstone – Born 1929

I was born in Liverpool in 1929. My family lived in a lovely council house in Norris Green and as well as my parents, I had one brother, Bert, and a lovely little baby sister, Estelle, who unfortunately died in 1983, the same year as my mother. My parents lived in the same house until they died.

Both my parents were born in England, but my grandparents originally escaped from Russia in the late 1800s. They lived in a small village outside Odessa, and when I was small my grandmother told me stories about the pogroms and persecution and how most of the villages were burnt down by the Cossacks. My grandparents were very young when they emigrated; she was sixteen years old and my grandfather was eighteen. I often think about how awful it must have been for them travelling through countries with all their belongings on a hand-pulled cart. However, they eventually arrived in London and settled in Brick Lane, where, a short time later, my mother was born. So my grandmother was pregnant and trying to escape, that would be a story in itself.

I have often tried to trace their origins, but, as they spoke very little English, the trend was to give the immigrants the first name they mentioned, and I was always under the impression that my grandfather took my grandmother's maiden name of Caplan, trying to remain incognito to escape persecution.

At last they arrived in Liverpool and, although their intention was to go on to America, as most immigrants did at that time, they stayed in the city. They did not speak the same language and had no money, but somehow, they managed to start a business. Grandfather started to collect secondhand goods with a handcart, and from there, built up a successful antiques business. From that beginning, his successors in the family started a general shop in Soho Street and then on to other retail shops. The original antiques shop is still standing at the corner of Stafford Street and Islington, and is now a general shop. There were eight children in all and my mother was the eldest.

The family moved to a house over a shop in Islington, which is where they lived at the beginning of the war. My Uncle Louis Caplan, who was the next to youngest child, became the Lord Mayor of Liverpool from 1964 to 1965. He was known as the 'Beatles' Lord Mayor'. Each time the Beatles are

One of the many slogans coined by the Government during the war was 'Make Do and Mend'. At the end of the war, women, couldn't wait to dress up in the 'New Look'. Tina's father was a tailor, so he was able to make her one of the new dresses with the flattering full skirt and tight waist.

shown on television, there is usually a clip taken on the balcony of the Town Hall showing my aunt and uncle with the Beatles, so they are not forgotten and it is great to see them again. The Lady Mayoress was his sister, my Aunt Fanny. So, out of a traumatic and humble beginning, he rose to this very proud position and it is sad that his parents did not live to see it.

At the age of five I started school at Leamington Road, Norris Green. Being the only Jewish child in the school, I did not go into assembly and instead gave the milk out to all the classrooms while the other children were at prayers. I hated this job as the milk always spilt and stained my dress which made me feel even more different – I already suffered from the bigotry which was very prevalent in my early years.

I was ten when the war started and my earliest memory, or at least my most vivid, was being in a shelter in the garden in the middle of an air-raid. I remember being terrified of the whistling bombs and also being dressed, as were my brother and sister, in an itchy 'siren suit', as they were called. They were made out of khaki, as my father, who was a tailor, made uniforms during the war for the Army and the Navy, so obviously the materials were offcuts. Well we hope so ...

My mother looked after one of the family general shops in Soho Street. We had a wonderful offer from my Aunt Gert and Uncle Abe who lived in Farsley between Bradford and Leeds, who suggested that they would love to look after us. I was delighted, but my brother was not as keen and my sister was only a baby. So I ended up staying with my aunt and uncle, and was very spoilt as they did not have a daughter and they treated me as their own. I stayed there for about four years and went to the village school in Farsley. Mum, Dad, Bert and Estelle used to visit often, so it was a happy time for me and while I was there I passed my Eleven Plus examination. Unfortunately my aunt fell ill and, at fourteen, I had to return to Liverpool where, thankfully, the bombing had stopped.

After the war, in 1947, fashion for women changed dramatically. The end of austerity was marked by the glamorous 'New Look' - full skirts and slim waists – created by Christian Dior. After years of wearing overalls and service uniforms women could not wait to be seen in these flatteringly feminine clothes. My father, being a tailor, made me a beautiful New Look coat and a 'long line' suit with a fitted skirt, in a gorgeous shade of blue. I really felt 'chic', to use a French word which was popular at the time. At about this

The top portrait of Tina, aged three, was taken at Dobson's of Bold Street.

Tina aged nine.

time my parents sent me to the Art School in Liverpool. My favourite part of these studies was learning to sketch and doing scenes involving lots of light and shade. Looking back I regret not concentrating more on my studies.

When my two aunts decided to marry (one went to Holland, the other to London), my grandmother and my two uncles were left to fend for themselves and my mother insisted that I look after them. I accepted this arrangement and moved in with them. I tried my best to cook for them but I had some terrible disasters. Fortunately I became friendly with a caterer and his family who lived opposite and one of his daughters would come over and show me what to do. Thank heaven for that, I eventually became a good cook.

Looking after my uncles was not always hard work. My Uncle Louis was at that time getting involved with politics and he would often bring colleagues home for lunch. Through him I was able to meet some famous and interesting people. Bessie and Jack Braddock would often visit the house and I well remember meeting Tony Benn and Fenner Brockway all those years ago. I was also lucky enough to visit the House of Commons many times.

I married at nineteen to a friend of my Uncle Max, who was much older than me. Looking back I honestly think I married to escape the household chores and gain a bit of independence. I was thrilled to have my own home, but thereby hangs another long story.

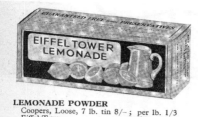
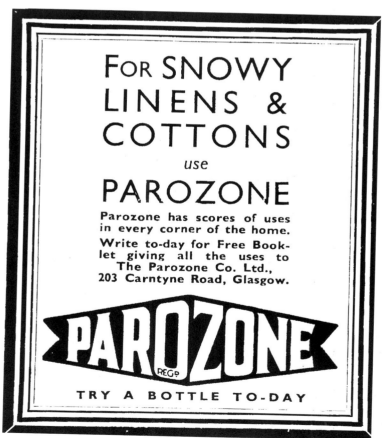

Barbara Harrison – Born 1932

I was born in Mill Road Maternity Hospital, Liverpool on 2 July 1932, the only girl in a family of six children. My family name was McAdam. I had lots of aunties and uncles who all lived within streets of each other in a very close-knit community off Townsend Lane in Anfield. Along with most other men at this time, my father was out of work a lot. He would get an odd day's work filling coal sacks, until he was finally given a full time job as a coalman. This made life a little easier for my mother.

Most of my childhood was spent playing in Breckside Park. In the thirties the park was the heart of our community, with well kept tennis courts and bowling greens that children were not allowed to set foot upon. Mums would sit around on doorsteps chatting, while children played rounders, skipping, top and whip and many other street games. Elallio was a favourite game and could involve any number of people. It was really an elaborate form of hide and seek in which the 'man' would hunt for the others and when he captured someone, he would shout 'elallio' and take them to his den. Sometimes mums and dads would join in the games. Such games are impossible today because of the volume of traffic on our congested streets, but in those days they helped to keep us fit!

Summers in the 1930s seemed endless, maybe it was because I was young and carefree, but life seemed so happy with lots of simple but exciting things happening, like the Hi li man who would come to the park each summer. All the local children would gather round him and compete with each other with a wooden bat and a ball on elastic – whoever kept it going the longest would win a Mars Bar.

Although I loved the summer most, winter evenings could be cosy, sitting round the fire with my brothers playing Ludo and Snakes and Ladders, while mum and dad listened to the radio. Sometimes we would all play cards or do jigsaws together. Then it would be off to bed with either the oven shelf or a hot brick to warm the beds.

One thing I did not enjoy doing was being sent by my mum to the Co-op to fetch the groceries. There was always a long queue of people waiting while the assistants laboriously weighed out all the goods and sliced the bacon to order and usually had a conversation with the older customers. I

A woman's work certainly was never done. Not only did they have to do all their housework without the help of any mod cons, but it was also a point of pride that the outside of their houses had to be kept scrubbed and spotless. Donkey stoning the front step and keeping the windows clean were frequent chores.

Barbara, aged two, wearing a hand-knitted dress.

Going to the cinema was extremely popular in the 1930s and 40s and a trip to one of Liverpool's many 'Dream Palaces' provided an escape into a different and infinitely more glamorous world.

still remember our Co-op number, which had to be given in, in order to receive the dividend. This would be saved up to be spent at Christmas. Most people in those days survived by using Sturla's or Co-op cheques, or pawning clothes, bedding or other household goods. We were very lucky because we had very good neighbours who would help each other out.

The food we ate in the 1930s was very plain but healthy. Many of the dishes we ate I would not dream of eating today, such as sheep's head broth. I would often come home from school to find a sheep's head soaking in a bowl of water to remove the blood. This was not in any way an off-putting or gruesome sight. On the contrary, it meant that we were in for a treat; sheep's head broth with dumplings – lovely! Homemade brawn was another favourite. Every butcher sold pigs' heads, and at least once a week mum would buy one. I never actually saw her make it but the end result would be a basin full of brawn that we would eat on top of a pile of homemade chips. It would melt all over them and tasted delicious.

We also loved such things as pig's feet and belly, tripe and onions and rabbit soup – still a favourite of mine today. We did not have much fruit, but mum would sometimes give us a few coppers to go to the greengrocers to buy a bag of 'fades', or damaged fruit. She would stew it all up together and serve it with custard, which was a real treat.

Toast was made by holding the bread on a toasting fork against the bars of the fire. I don't know if bread was better then, but toast has never tasted so good since. At Christmas mum would bake a large bunloaf which I would take to our local bakery, Kelly's, on Townsend Lane, who would cook all the bunloaves for all the local families, who, like mine, had no stove; everything was cooked on the open fire.

In the 1930s and 1940s, people who were lucky enough to be employed worked very long hours, and those who were out of work would have very little money, so entertainment, a form of escape, was very important to everyone. Every area had many small picture houses. I lived in the Anfield area and the local cinemas were the Cabbage Hall (now Liverpool Supporters' Club), the Lido, which became a club called the Wooky Hollow, the Ritz, which became a bingo hall and the Clubmoor and the Royal, which are now furniture shops.

There were so many picture houses in Liverpool, that the whole front page of the *Liverpool Echo* would be full of advertisements for them. Being one of the main forms of entertainment, the cinemas were always full; in fact most nights there would be long queues outside. Saturday afternoon was usually reserved for children, when they could go in without an adult. This was the highlight of the week for the children of our area. Children whose parents were broke would run round their neighbours' houses to see if anyone had a lemonade bottle to give them. These could be taken back to the sweet shop, where the child would be given twopence – enough to get into the Saturday matinee. There was always a serial showing, such as *Flash Gordon, The Clutching Hand*, or a cowboy film. These always ended in a cliff-hanger and we would spend the next week speculating on how the hero or heroine could survive, and, of course, they always did.

As I reached my teens in the 1940s, I still enjoyed going to the cinema,

but dancing became my favourite pastime. Most church halls would hold small dances for the local young people. My favourite venue was the Hamilton Road Mission, where one of the priests would always be present, probably to ensure that there was no 'hanky panky'. The only records played there were Victor Sylvester dance records. We had a great time there dancing the legs off ourselves. On the way home we would all pile into the local milk bar to have a Vantas drink before going home at 10pm, tired but happy.

As I reached my mid-teens, I started venturing further afield. A visit to the Odeon, the Futurist, or the Forum, in town, was a real big night out and I would feel very adventurous. When I finally made it to the larger dance halls such as the Grafton, Blairs and Burtons, I felt that I was really living. Dancing to some of the big bands of the day such as Joe Loss and Ivy Benson was a real thrill. Just after the Second World War, lots of American soldiers who were based around Merseyside would visit the Grafton; this is when dancing really started to come alive with the Jive being one of the most popular dances. This was one of the most exciting times of my life, but of course, maybe it seemed this way because I was young. But, I cannot believe that young people today have as much fun as we had in those days.

On 3 September 1939, the war started and I, along with my brothers and

"We would emerge after the 'all clear' full of apprehension. Sometimes we would find the area we lived in badly damaged by bombs and people we knew had been killed. It was soul destroying, but looking back it was amazing how people pulled together and helped each other out."

most other children in our neighbourhood were evacuated to Wales. I was placed in two different homes and was very unhappy in both. The first placement was with a doctor and his wife who made it quite obvious that they did not want evacuees. Two of us were put with this couple and the other girl fretted so much that she was taken back to Liverpool. On her first day home she was in an air-raid shelter along with her family during a raid. The shelter suffered a direct hit and they were all killed. I was told about this but still cried to go home. Instead I was moved to another part of Wales, to an even worse place – the home of a nurse and her blind father. I had to sit in the dark with him each night while she was at work. I was treated like a skivvy and was relieved when my mother arrived to take me home.

When the air-raids were at their height, we slept in the air-raid shelter in our backyard. Liverpool was very badly bombed and the raids were terrifying; the noise absolutely deafening. Sleeping in the air-raid shelter was quite scary, it was very cramped and dark and smelled strongly of mould and damp. There were two bunks beds at one end and a larger bed on the floor. We had candles and torches but it was still very gloomy, but at least it kept us safe.

We kept ourselves amused and tried to take our minds off what was happening outside by playing word games, this did not take away the fear but it gave a strong feeling of togetherness. We would emerge after the 'all clear' full of apprehension. Sometimes we would find the area we lived in badly damaged by bombs and people we knew had been killed. It was soul destroying, but looking back it was amazing how people pulled together and helped each other out.

People also had to live with the constant, gnawing worry of sons, husbands and daughters in the Armed Forces. They had waved goodbye to them, not knowing when, or if, they would ever see them again. The *Liverpool Echo* would print lists of people missing, or killed in action and sometimes the name of a person from our neighbourhood would appear. The telegraph boy was all too often the bringer of bad tidings and a communal shiver would go through the street when he was seen taking bad news to a neighbour's house. On such occasions, everyone would rally round and help in whatever way they could, relieved that, for now, their own loved ones were safe.

There was a barrage balloon station on Breckside Park and it was a common occurrence to see tanks rattling and creaking up and down our street. We soon got used to them and felt safer knowing they were there. Despite all the difficulties brought by the war, it was still much better being at home than living far away in Wales.

My father was in the Merchant Navy during the war and my mother worked in a pub. The lady whose house we shared looked after the family and became like a grandmother to my brothers and me.

The school I attended before the war was the 'tin' school in Townsend lane, so-called because it was constructed of corrugated iron. I am not sure

The top photograph of Barbara aged five, was taken on Empire Day in 1937.

Barbara as a young woman.

Parcels for His Majesty's Forces at Home and Abroad

IF you are sending parcels, we suggest a visit to the Home and Overseas Parcel Section. Here are displayed the most suitable items for despatch, and full information relative to postage, packing, etc., is available. If, however, you cannot call, and will advise us, a list of suggested parcels will be sent by post, together with particulars regarding Duty Free Cigarettes and Tobacco.

C O O P E R S

CHURCH STREET . . LIVERPOOL, 1

TELEPHONE ROYAL SIX THOUSAND

Men serving abroad during the war had precious few luxuries to help them survive their ordeal, and a parcel from home was a huge boost to morale.

what happened to it, but it disappeared after the evacuation. One of my early memories of school is of May Day, when most children would dress up in red, white and blue clothing. We would dance around the maypole after crowning the May Queen. All the girls desperately wanted to be picked to be the May Queen. I was never chosen, but I did once become her train bearer, which made me feel very important. After school we would often dress up in old net curtains and have our own May procession in the street. We would also hold concerts in the backyard and charge a halfpenny to watch.

The remainder of my school days were spent at Pinehurst Avenue Junior School and Stanley Park Senior School. I left when I was fourteen, in 1946, and went to work in Ogden's Tobacco Factory. While working in Ogden's I met Fred Harrison who was to become my husband. He was twenty and I was seventeen when we met in 1950, and we married in 1953.

Margaret Gillin – Born 1932

I was born in Liverpool in 1932, therefore what memories I have of the 1930s are of childhood, and the events I recall are as seen through the eyes of a child. My father was a docker, which at that time was classed as casual work. I was the ninth child in the family and my parents were to have another two after me, eleven children in all, seven girls and four boys.

The house in which I was born was rather small and was situated within rows and rows of similar houses in the West Derby Road area. There was no bathroom in the house and the toilet was in the back yard. Our water was heated on the fire, or on the small gas cooker in the kitchen, we also had a brick boiler in the kitchen, which my mother would have to light with paper and wood, before she began the enormous task of washing all the clothes.

As a child I was not aware of how poor we were, my early memories are of warmth and laughter; the realisation of poverty came later, when I noticed other children's clothes and toys. Most mornings I awoke to the sound of my mother singing. I was to learn later that many a morning she sang knowing that she did not have a single penny in her purse.

In 1937, I started at St Michael's school in York Street. I remember being quite happy about it, because my brother and two of my sisters were already there. Another reason was that in those days of large families, there were always other children from the street starting at the same time. Charlie from next door and Frankie who lived four doors down, started along with me. However, by playtime on the first day, Frankie decided that he had had enough education and took himself off home. Our teacher asked if anyone knew where he lived, and being a little busybody, I put up my hand and offered to go and bring him back. The teacher agreed and I duly went to fetch him. How times have changed; a teacher would lose her job today if she sent an infant on such an errand, never mind one who had only started that morning! Frankie went on to win a scholarship, learned to speak several languages, and worked at the United Nations, all due to me, (or so I like to think!).

In May of the same year we had a street party for the Coronation of George V1. However, the highlight of that week for me was the arrival of a baby brother. I was delighted, as any five-year-old would be, but I don't think

This photo appeared in the Liverpool Echo in September 1939 and shows a group of evacuees, packed and ready for their journey to North Wales. As for many others, life for Margaret was never to be the same again after she returned from the evacuation.

This cobbled 1930s street, showing just a few of the children who lived there, is typical in having a corner shop selling general groceries. Notice the white, donkey-stoned steps in front of every doorway.

my older sisters were too pleased at the idea of yet another baby arriving on the scene – my sister Vera had been born only two years earlier.

Towards the end of the thirties my parents started taking Vera and I to the pictures, to see the Shirley Temple films. There were quite a few cinemas in our area, all within walking distance. The Hippodrome, Savoy and Palladium were all in West Derby Road, and the Cosy was in Boaler Street. As we got older, we used to wonder why my father did not seem to mind watching these children's films. We came to realise that Shirley always had one of the top male dancers of the time appearing with her. Stars like Buddy Epson, and Bill (Bojangles) Robinson, were entertainers in their own right, and this was an opportunity for my father, and indeed others who loved dancing, to see them.

Shirley Temple was quite a phenomenon throughout the 1930s. Many girls born in that decade were called after her, and she certainly set the trend in clothes, for those who could afford them. Two of my older sisters who were now working bought Vera and myself Shirley Temple dresses, much to my disgust as I was a tomboy. They had box pleats that started from the yoke, and were just not suitable for playing in the street, not the sort of games we played then, rounders, top and whip and bursting shiny black tar bubbles that appeared in the street in the warm weather.

It was the Cosy picture house that we 'bunked' into a few years later, I was about ten and Vera was eight. This was quite a common escapade then; children would find various ways of getting into the pictures without paying, so we decided to give it a try.

We managed to climb through the ground floor window of the ladies toilet and then nonchalantly walked into the foyer.

"Who brought you in?" asked the usherette, eyeing us suspiciously.

"Er, some women in a green hat," replied our Vera, trying edge me towards the auditorium.

She grabbed us both by the collar like two bank robbers and pushed us into the stalls. She then shone her torch all around, there was not a hat to be seen, green or otherwise.

"Sit there," she said, through gritted teeth, "I'm sending for the police."

We sat petrified, turning around in terror every time the door opened, expecting to see the entire Liverpool police force coming to take us away. When the film ended we bolted out of the exit and ran like the wind all the way home. Neither of us can remember the name of the film, or what it was about, such was our fright, and there was no more bunking in for us.

As children we only ever received toys at Christmas, so we used to get very excited when the ragman came round offering a cheap toy in exchange for some rags. One day I saw the ragman trundling his cart down the street calling, "Rag and bones, rag and bones" and I could not control the urge to somehow get myself a toy. So I dashed into the house and snatched my sister Julia's coat off the hook in the lobby; she was on her dinner hour from Ogden's. The ragman took the coat from me without question and handed me a balloon. There was complete uproar in the house when my 'crime' was discovered. I still have a mental picture of my poor mother running along the road as if her life depended on it, chasing after the ragman, with the balloon bobbing up and down behind her. Then the frantic tug of war that followed, as she angrily pulled the coat off the cart.

In 1938 my brother Tom joined the Army and when he came home on leave at Christmas, we had a party. As things turned out, it was to be the last Christmas that the family would spend together. I well remember my sisters and brothers and their friends dancing to the latest Joe Loss record and the fun we had together.

September 1939 saw the start of one of the worst periods in history, with families across the country torn apart by war. My family's sadness was to begin six months earlier, when my brother Andrew tragically died of peritonitis. He had become ill with severe stomach pains and the doctor was called. He diagnosed indigestion and prescribed some medicine. His condition worsened overnight and another doctor was called (this could happen then, provided you paid a fee). My brother was immediately taken to Mill Road Infirmary, where my parents were told that his appendix had burst, causing peritonitis, and there was nothing that could be done. Andrew died the following day. He was only twenty-three years old and was the eldest of my parents' children. From a child's point of view, I can only dimly recall the feeling of sadness that hung heavily over the house like a mist, but what I can remember is that my mother never sang again, well not for a long, long time.

As a seven-year-old in 1939, I do not remember being too upset when I heard that there was going to be a war, but I do remember the excitement at the thought of the evacuation. I was to be sent away with my brother Joe, who was just coming up to his eleventh birthday, and my sister Vera who was five years old. The children of that time can be excused for not taking the news of the outbreak of the war seriously, we just had no idea of what to expect. We had not been fed on a diet of war films, showing all the horror that war brings, like today's generation of children. The most violent scenes

Remember When ...

Miscellaneous

- An ice cart that delivered blocks of ice to meat and fish shops.

- Tram drivers worked exposed to all the elements with no shelter.

- There was a post box on the back of the last tram. Letters, bearing a penny halfpenny stamp, would be delivered next morning.

- People relied on the factory hooters and the one o'clock gun to tell them the time.

- Schoolteachers and midwives often rode bikes but, for modesty's sake, they attached a piece of elastic to the hem of their skirt and looped it over their foot.

- A horse drawn merry-go-round came round the streets now and then and children could have a ride in exchange for a jam jar.

- Children used to enjoy bursting tar bubbles in the road on hot days.

- The Indian toffee man used to come round selling delicious golden spun toffee.

The 'Wonda' Washing Copper – a very early and crude type of washing machine.

Every kitchen in the 1930s had a mangle – the only way to wring water out of the week's washing.

I remember watching were the 'Three Stooges' as they twisted each other's noses, pulled Curley's hair out almost by the roots, or hit someone with a plank! The only 'war' films we watched were cowboys and Indians, and even then I watched with my hands over my eyes when the arrows were flying about.

We were evacuated to a small farm in Ellesmere, Shropshire. The nearest village was Techil, where we went to school. It was mainly a poultry farm but the farmer also kept a few cows and there was also an orchard. It was autumn, and the apples and pears were ripe, and we thought we were in heaven being able to eat as much fruit as we liked. We were allowed to help on the farm, feeding the chickens, collecting the eggs and bringing the vegetables in from the garden for dinner. Joe also cleaned out the cowshed and I helped in the house by washing the dishes and brushing the floor. The farmer and his wife treated us very well, but the homesickness became unbearable, and the novelty of the farm and country life soon wore off.

The timing of our homecoming could not have been worse because we arrived back in Liverpool just before the terrible bombing in December 1940, during which a landmine was dropped at the top of our street (Goldsmith Street) killing many people. Another landmine hit our local hospital, Mill Road, in 1941, when ninety-two people died, including patients, staff and ambulance drivers.

Our education at this time was almost non-existent, schools were closed in some areas, because the teachers were still away with the evacuees. Our school did not re-open fully until 1943. We were taught at a private house for just one afternoon a week.

The bombsites soon became our playgrounds; new areas to explore and search for buried 'treasure'. When the sewing factory in Farnworth street was bombed, we spent hours happily digging through the debris for reels of cotton and buttons.

Many children played a vital role during the war years; with mothers now working in munitions factories, it was left to the older children to collect their brothers and sisters from the nursery schools, and care for them until their mothers came home from work. When school resumed, we also collected 'salvage' from the shops, we would run along West Derby Road in our dinner hour with a sack, calling in at all the shops for scrap paper, cardboard and empty tins. This would all be stored at the school until it was collected for recycling by the council. We really felt as though we were helping the war effort and so did the Lord Mayor at the time, for he invited two children from each school to visit the Town Hall and gave us a pound each in recognition of our efforts.

During the air-raids, my family and neighbours hurried for shelter in a large reinforced cellar under Little's Piano Shop, at the corner of our street. The shelter was well lit and had bunk beds along the wall, and there was plenty of room for us children to play. The women used to sing to keep their spirits up and some of them had lovely singing voices, I can still remember many of the songs they sang.

A great pastime for us children was waiting for the old women to fall asleep, which they would do sitting upright in their chairs. We would creep up on them and watch closely as they started to snore, causing their entire face and neck to shudder. Sometimes they woke themselves up if they gave an extra loud snore, sending us scattering in all directions, in case they realised what we were up to. The times we spent in the shelter were by no means always miserable, and we were too young to realise the full horror of what was happening up above.

In 1942 my youngest brother John was killed by a lorry, he was just five years old. He too could be classed as a war casualty; children were not used to the heavy traffic which began to trundle noisily from the docks in a steady stream, to the munitions factories which were dotted around the city. My parents, like millions of others, had to try and cope with the terrible loss. More and more families were receiving tragic news of their loved ones from the front. Whenever a telegraph boy appeared, a hush would descend over the street. The women would stop what they were doing, and freeze, almost like statues, dreading that the telegram would be for them.

Throughout the war years life seemed to go on; a thin veneer of normality spread over the awful reality. People made the most of things, they still laughed and sang and went to the pictures or to a dance. Young people still met and fell in love and when possible, got married. West Derby Road was a hive of activity then, because of the Grafton, which was a popular dance hall. I remember seeing lots of American servicemen going to the dances and they were very generous with their chewing gum, giving it to any children that were around, especially if they were cheeky enough to ask "Got any gum, chum?".

I was thirteen when the war ended, a feeling of relief and hope swept over the family, but that feeling only lasted a short time, because, two months later, my father died. There were three of us still at school. Life at home was never the same again. Six months after he died I left school at the age of fourteen. As my mother only received a pension of ten shillings, and five shillings for my sister, I had to take the job which paid the most money.

My first job was in a sewing factory, making belt loops for men's overalls, and my wages were just under a pound a week. My meagre pocket money was soon spent, which did not bother me too much, because all my friends were in a similar situation. We would find things to do that did not cost much money, such as going for a sail across to Seacombe and walking to New Brighton, where we would buy a bag of chips. We also went to town to gaze into the shop windows, choosing all the things that we promised ourselves when we were rich. Dancing was also very popular. As well as the big dance halls like the Grafton and the Rialto, there were lots of smaller places that we could go to in our own area. Many churches ran dances, there was even some tuition available, and someone would always show you the different steps and variations.

Another favourite pastime was cycling; as well as it being a pleasure, many people also cycled to work. Secondhand bikes could be bought quite cheaply, and after a coat of paint, and perhaps a new bell, we really did feel as though we owned the road. How wonderful it was then, in the late 1940s and early 1950s, cycling every Sunday to one of the many beauty spots, or places of interest, that are within easy reach of Liverpool. The eight o'clock

ferry from Woodside would be full of cyclists all heading for North Wales. Soon, however, the motor car took over and the roads became too busy. Cycling was never quite the same again.

Holidays abroad were beyond our means, but my friends and I did go to the Isle of Man and Ireland, but only after saving up all year round. There was also a Government-sponsored scheme entitled 'Lend a Hand on the Land', which was looked upon as a type of holiday. It was possible to travel to various rural areas and work on the farms there for a week. The scheme proved to be very popular, giving people the opportunity to travel to different parts of the country.

Our accommodation was in converted Army huts, which were quite comfortable, and it was all quite a novelty for us. After breakfast we were given a packed lunch, and then taken to a farm to work for the day. The work varied, from gathering in the harvest to hoeing. We were not worked too hard and it was all a lot of fun – so different from our work in the factories and offices back home and what is more, we got paid for it.

Our evenings would be spent in the village pub, gathering around the piano, singing the latest songs from the 'Hit Parade'. I remember Hoagie Carmichael being in the charts at that time. We usually drank shandies, but on one occasion a few of us tried the local cider, but only the once, as it was so strong.

I look back on these, my teenage years, as happy and carefree. Courtship and a happy marriage and motherhood were in the not too distant future. I did not know it then, but the best was yet to come.

Lily Jones – Born 1932

In September 1939 the war arrived. I was seven years of age. Strangely enough, for many people it meant that at long last they could obtain work! Women were suddenly in demand as well as men, so financially at least, it meant a better life in some ways.

On one of those glorious sunny days that herald the end of summer, I was sitting on the pavement with a group of my pals. We were all intently prising out the strips of green moss from between the paving stones with sticks. Anyone watching us would not have guessed that we needed the moss for a specific purpose – to play shop with. But no one was watching us because, suddenly, all the adults started pouring out of the houses, talking loudly and urgently. We stopped what we were doing and studied the faces of our mums and dads. There was a palpable air of worry, discord, and unrest and it then was explained to us – war had just been declared and they had all heard it on the radio.

At the start of the war, everyone was concerned with more mundane practicalities: the building of air-raid shelters, the introduction of identity cards and ration-books which were issued for food, clothing and petrol. Petrol coupons were only issued to essential workers, but few people owned cars anyway. The blitz to us children became just a part of normal everyday life, but to the adults it must have been a terrifying experience. There were the warning sirens ... the drone of bombers and fighters overhead ... the terrible noise of the ack-ack (anti-aircraft) guns ... the flashes of the guns and the exploding bombs ... the night skies lit up with the criss-crossing search-lights ... and the ping of the falling shrapnel! Yes, I remember all of that.

A squad of soldiers was billeted on the Gandy field near where we lived. We children went to watch them putting up their huge bell-tents and field kitchen. They were filling little sacks with sand, one of them gave me a sixpence for holding the sacks out whilst he filled them. They were in charge of two barrage-balloons, we thought they looked like great wobbly elephants in the sky, and we loved to watch them being reeled in, or raised up into the sky from the trucks to which they were tethered. Once or twice we saw a free-flying 'dumbo' which had broken away from its mooring wire! The balloons were used as a defence against low-flying aircraft, but, as far as I

A visit to the cinema was a regular treat during the 1930s and 40s, enjoyed by all ages.

During the war, in the interests of security, everyone had to carry an identity card and produce it when requested.

know, no enemy planes were brought down by the ones in our field.

The roads were festooned with metal pipes, for emergency water supply, and also with ramps at the end of the roads so that vehicles could enter or leave without damaging the pipes. The windows in every building were criss-crossed with brown sticky paper to help stop flying glass in the event of bomb blast. And all the windows had to be fitted with blackout curtains – not a chink of light had to be shown!

Most boys and girls collected the shrapnel that fell everywhere, and vied with each other as to who had the largest pieces. We often went to the air-raid shelter in the basement of Wallasey Town Hall, I vividly remember sitting on a top bunk swinging my legs and boasting that I was going for a trip to West Kirby the next day, by electric train. There were sing-songs when the raids were on, to cheer people up and block out the sound of the bombs. There was laughter as well as tears. Life went on. We were taken on trips to the Liverpool shops and to West Kirby as well.

My school at Somerville was badly damaged and for a time we had to share with the children of St Joseph's, or as we called it, St Joey's. I was greatly intrigued with the sheet-covered statues of saints in the corner of each classroom, and asked my mother why they were there. She did not seem to know, but I suppose they were to protect them from any bomb blast. We attended for a few half-days only during the period of the worst blitzes in May 1940.

My teacher, Miss Humphries, was a real old dragon, I was terrified of her! She was one of the old retired teachers who were brought back to work because many of the younger ones were doing more important things for the war effort. According to her, all the people in Africa lived in grass huts and all Americans were cowboys, and everybody in Canada lived in an igloo! All through the war years we children enjoyed our third of a pint of fresh milk each morning, provided free by the Government. We drank it in the mid-morning break and in the cold winter months there was usually a slice of delicious ice underneath the cardboard cap. To be chosen as milk-monitor was considered a much prized job.

On one occasion Miss Humphries told us that she had a surprise for us and she produced a pile of parcels, one for each of us. Apparently they were gifts from children in America. We were each given one of the parcels. There were books, dolls and other toys. I was given a book and was rather disappointed. I looked enviously at those children who had been given toys.

My brother, Bill, was a cabin boy on the Empress ships which travelled backwards and forwards to Canada and then were used as troop-ships throughout the war. Each time he came home to Merseyside he always brought wonderful things for the family; fruit, chocolate, magazines for mum and comics for me and 'Lifesavers', which were fruit sweets shaped like Polos. He also brought me an American raincoat, which was designed to look like an American fire-fighter's rain gear, with a helmet-type hat attached. I was very proud of it. Bill was only sixteen or so at the time.

My older brother, George, worked on the railways for LNER and although he wanted to join the Navy, he was not allowed to, as his job was classed as essential work. After a few months he was posted to Tredegar, in

South Wales, where he spent the rest of the war years as a fireman on the steam locomotives which hauled coal to the factories in that area.

My sister Hannah joined the ATS (Auxilliary Territorial Service), and after being trained at Pontefract, was posted to Folkestone as a cook in a hotel which was used as a base for soldiers returning from war zones. She had some fine tales to tell of all the things she and the other girls got up to! For instance, on one occasion they went to a dance in an Army ambulance with all the bells ringing so they could get there faster. When she came home on leave she would always take me over to Liverpool on the ferry, for a meal and a visit to the cinema, usually the Odeon, which had a Hammond organ which rose up out of the floor, playing for singsongs. She also would buy me a new dress or coat. Looking back I now realise what a pittance they both received and understand just how generous they were.

My dear old dad was a donkey-man (winchman) on the docks all through the blitz. He worked the little steam-driven winches on the decks of the ships, which hauled the cargoes in and out of the holds. He always boasted that he was so skilful with the winches that he could crack an egg with them! The docks, of course, were a prime target for the German bombers, but the dockers worked right through the air-raids and dashed home when they could to check that their families were safe. Once my dad had to go out to the Mersey Bar to remove ammunition from a badly damaged ship – a difficult and dangerous mission – so he was one of the many unsung heroes of the war. There was no official recognition for their hard work and no special equipment or protective clothing was issued to them. In winter the dockers wore much the same clothes as they did in summer. Dad had served in the Cheshire Regiment in the First World War and was stationed in Greece, near Salonica. He worked until he was seventy and retired without anything from the Dock Board, just his ordinary state pension. Not even a thankyou.

The only member of our family to suffer an injury in the blitz was a cousin, Jackie Henshaw. He was standing in the doorway of his papershop, in Wheatland Lane, when a bomb-blast shattered the glass door, amputating his right arm near the shoulder. He lived for many years after the war and seemed to manage quite well. As a family we were very lucky, as in Wallasey alone, 358 citizens were killed, and in total, 5,616 people died on Merseyside. I went with my mother to a mass burial at Rake Lane cemetery, the huge grave is situated by the railings, opposite the rear of Earlston Library. There is also a memorial stone.

During the war there were huge black painted metal containers in nearly all the roads in the town. These held emergency water supplies for fire fighting and were about five feet high. They had EWS painted in white on the side. There were also large, brick-built, air-raid shelters in many of the terraced streets, because their yards were not big enough to hold an Anderson shelter.

Some of the Birkenhead buses towed a gas-cylinder behind them on a trailer, replacing petrol, which was scarce. Birkenhead buses were blue, Wallasey buses were yellow and Liverpool trams and buses were painted dark green. The headlamps were covered in black paint except for a little cross that

Lily with her mother. The cotton overall which her mother is wearing is very typical of the 1940s.

allowed a glimmer of light to show through. All the street lamps were out of use completely, and air-raid wardens were always checking for chinks of escaping light. "Put that light out!" was their continual cry and it became standing joke. So, on moonless nights, getting about was very difficult.

One of the Wallasey ferryboats was bombed and sank at the Seacombe landing stage and the funnel stuck out of the river for a few years before the boat was finally salvaged. There used to be very dense, choking fogs in those days, because everyone used coal for heating. So when the fog was thick, a cacophony of hooters and ships' bells would come from the river, which was always full of shipping. The river was an exciting place and it was always an event to travel to Liverpool by ferry to go shopping.

People learned to queue for everything and queuing became a habit that is now regarded as a British tradition. Ration days came once a week, when the family's rations were bought from the local Co-op in Borough Road, where my family was registered. We usually had a delicious meal of bacon and eggs on that day. If people were lucky enough to have a garden, they would keep a flock of hens and feed them on boiled potato peelings, and anything else they could lay their hands on, so that they could supplement their meagre rations with fresh eggs – a valuable source of protein.

My family was blitzed out of Oakland Avenue and moved to Poulton. The house we moved to was not much better, as all the windows had been replaced with plasterboard, except for the middle ones! The school opposite had a wing completely bombed out of existence. It was a very hard cold winter that year, the pipes were all frozen solid, and so most of our neighbours obtained their water in buckets from the school's boiler-room in the basement.

People generally only had a single fire in their main living room, which also heated the water in a back boiler. The bedrooms were usually icy cold, as was all the rest of the house, until a fire was lit each morning. Coal was delivered by horse and cart, as was the milk. Spragg, the farmer from Breck Road, delivered milk to the Poulton area in a churn on a cart. His farm was where the motorway bridge is now. Household scraps were put into pig-bins, which were chained to the lampposts. We always knew when Mr Spragg had arrived, because his pony was adept at knocking off the lid of our pig-bin for a little snack! The scraps were collected and distributed to farms on the Wirral; absolutely nothing was wasted. All the park railings disappeared at the start of the war, and people were also asked to contribute any pots and pans or any metallic articles they could spare to help the war-effort.

Very ordinary people were extremely brave during the blitz and many people were killed and injured in the air-raids, but there were always lighter moments. One time a rumour went around the Seacombe children that a boat in the docks was giving away Jaffa oranges. Troupes of children hurried down to the dock and the seamen and dockers threw down dozens of semi-rotten oranges to us. It must have been a refrigerated ship that had sustained damage on its voyage to Britain. The oranges tasted very good, because fruit was strictly rationed. Sweets were also in very short supply, so, to satisfy my sweet tooth, I sometimes bought cough-sweets from the chemist with my pocket money.

In St Pauls Road there was a community kitchen in an old church building, which has since been replaced by the Children's Resource Centre on the same site. It was run by the local council and, I suppose, by the WVS, or some other voluntary body. People who had been bombed out of their homes, or whose houses were damaged, could have a meal for very little money. It was open to anyone and it continued for some time after the war finally ended.

New Brighton was full of American troops prior to D Day. They were billeted in all the empty houses along and around Warren Drive, and in the empty hotels. There was also a motor-depot in the Palace indoor fairground, and most of the teenage girls and women enjoyed their company at the Tower Ballroom! I remember standing for ages at the top of Love Lane when they eventually left Wallasey in a seemingly never-ending convoy made up of all kinds of Army vehicles – we were sad to see them go.

Evidence of war was everywhere. Bomb sites transformed the landscape and soon, tall, red, rose-bay willow herb grew in profusion amongst the rubble. We called it 'bomb-site weed'. All along the north end of the peninsular, from Harrison Drive to Hoylake, were mined areas, which were fenced off and had notices warning of the danger. Perhaps the local militia hoped that the Germans could not read English! There were also pyramid-shaped tank-traps all along the embankment. Dad often used to take me for an early morning walk and we had to pass down to the shore through a narrow fenced path. He said he liked to get out before the streets were 'aired'. The sand-dunes were full of rabbits and nesting larks in those days. A singing lark always brings back memories of those sunny mornings with dad.

The overriding impressions I received as a child growing up in the thirties and during the period of wartime, were of darkness in the streets, noise and anxiety, being rushed into air-raid shelters in the early afternoons of the May Blitz, but also of happy family Christmases with home-made toys as presents ... wooden skittles, dolls' houses, brittle-papered books (the paper was made mostly from wood pulp) and shiny English apples at the bottom of our pillowslips. People helped each other out with food and also with their time, and were much kinder to each other than they are today.

The war eventually ended and I caught the New Brighton ferryboat with my mother, so that we could see all the lights reflecting in the river from the newly lit-up streets and buildings, quite a sight for me after experiencing five years of total blackout. Both Wallasey and Birkenhead ferries gave free trips up and down the river. Boats were hooting, bells were ringing and people were dancing in the streets and on the ferryboats.

Every street or road held a victory party. Long trestle tables were placed down the centre of the road, groaning with hoarded food and drink. Bunting was strung across the streets, pianos dragged out of houses and there were smiling, excited faces whichever way you looked. Bonfires were lit in the middle of the roads too.

Soon, fruit began to appear in the shops again. Some children had never seen a banana and had no idea how to tackle one. Rationing still continued, even though the war had been won, so there were still shortages. But everything gradually returned to normal. My brothers and sister came home to take up their lives again; George had picked up a faint Welsh accent, he had been away so long. I started senior school and ended up at the Wallasey College of Art in Central Park ... But that is another tale.

Be Sensible **AND YOU WILL BE SAFE**

THE LIGHT

IN THE DARK

upil is small
to exclude
much light

Pupil grows larger
to let in
more light

you go from light to black-out
E: let your eyes adjust themselves

HOLYROOD
for knitwear

Margaret McGarry – Born 1936

I was born in 1936 and lived in Hankin Street, at the junction of Scotland Road and Stanley Road. My father was a docker, and he later worked as a lorry driver. There were four children in the family; one boy, who was the eldest, and three girls.

My earliest memories are of the evacuation at the beginning of the war. We were evacuated along with other children from our parish to Penmaenmawr, on the North Wales coast. I remember crying at the thought of being separated from my brother Jimmy. He was taking care of me when the billeting officer suggested that we should be put with different families. My sister and I were to go to the local convent and my brother to the monastery but when I became upset it was agreed we should stay together. We were taken to stay in a lovely house with Mr and Mrs Roberts and their daughter. They made us very welcome and we soon settled in. Sadly, however, Mrs Roberts died eventually and we were then taken to live with a Mrs Hughes. This new arrangement did not last very long as I became ill with whooping cough and we had to return home.

I remember watching the air-raid shelters being built in the street, followed shortly afterwards by the heavy bombing. The Rotunda cinema was destroyed and the stables in Cranmer Street, which was at the back of Hankin Street, where the carters' horses were kept. The carters drove the horses and carts around the city, transporting goods from the dock warehouses to the factories and shops. Liverpool, being a large, busy port, made the carters a familiar sight on the city streets. Many of the present day haulage firms started their businesses this way. My grandfather was a master carter and had his own business (F Reid and Sons) owning many horses and carts. The carters had to go out, whatever the weather, putting sacks over their heads and shoulders for some little protection against the rain. They also took great pride in their horses, grooming them until their coats shone, then polishing the ornamental brasses on their manes until they were gleaming.

Two houses opposite our family home were also bombed. My school, St Gerard's, was another victim of the air-raids, which meant that the children of our parish had to attend St Sylvester's school instead. Even when the bombing was at its worst, I had great fun with all the other children on the

The blackout was very strictly enforced and getting about in the dark was very tricky. A Government slogan – 'Be seen, Be Safe' was backed up with advice on how to move about safely during the blackout.

street, playing and running in and out of the air-raid shelters, with the poor air-raid warden chasing after us. In spite of the bombing, our family still went to the pictures; we took turns going with mother. There were two picture houses near us in Scotland Road at that time, the Gaiety, which was demolished many years ago, and the Derby, which is now an undertakers.

When I was twelve, disaster struck the family when our mother died. She had been unwell for some weeks with bad headaches, which the doctor had put down to stress. On Easter Sunday she was admitted to hospital and my father was informed that she had a brain tumour. It was then found that she also had lung cancer and she was transferred to the radium hospital in Myrtle Street, where she remained for some weeks. Sadly, the doctors could do nothing to save her and she died in May, just eight weeks after her illness was diagnosed.

The shock of losing my mother was so great that I can barely remember her funeral, just that my brother and his friend were altar boys at the Requiem Mass and I remember thinking how brave they were. I also remember how upset I was the night before the funeral when I heard some of the visitors laughing. I wondered how they could be so callous, it didn't seem right when I was completely devastated. Much later in life I came to realise that they meant no harm, it was just their way of dealing with the family's grief.

The war had been over for three years and families everywhere were looking forward to things getting back to normal, but my family had to cope with this great sadness. Marie, who was the eldest girl, had won a scholarship to Everton Valley High School, but she gave up her studies to help look after the family; she was fifteen years old. This was an unselfish and courageous thing to do, as scholarships were not easy to achieve at this time. Boys in our younger days did not do any housework. It was not expected of them by either parent, nor were they encouraged to do what was considered to be women's work. Most girls were expected to wait on their brothers, cook a meal for them, or iron their clothes. Boys would do such 'manly' jobs as chopping wood for the fire and bringing in the coal.

I had many friends and was involved with numerous activities centred round our local church. I was in the junior Legion of Mary and also did voluntary work in the parish, visiting the elderly and doing housework for them. I also went to dances at St Anthony's and to a small dance hall called Bullens. I was never at home.

In 1951, when I was fifteen, I left St Sylvester's school and went to work in Aindows ice-cream factory in Carisbrooke Road. My wages were thirty shillings a week. Our working conditions were dreadful; we had to work in wellingtons, sloshing about in the cold and wet. There was no union to take our grievances to. My work involved taking the blocks of ice cream from the machine and it would then be sliced and packed in boxes. We girls were not allowed to feed the ingredients into the machine, the male employees did that.

Before we went home at night the machine would have to be hosed down and we used to get drenched – hence the wellingtons and the big rubber aprons we had to wear. The floor would also have to be cleaned and every Friday night the fridges had to be defrosted and cleaned. It was very hard work, the only compensation being that at least our feet were dry and we could eat as much ice cream as we liked. But as soon as I could I left Aindows and went to work as a junior Corris clerk in Littlewoods pools, where I stayed for two and a half years, when I had to leave for health reasons.

In 1952 the family moved to Croxteth, a new housing estate on the outskirts of Liverpool. It was so very different from the old neighbourhood. In 1957 I started work at AC Delco in Kirkby, the highlight of getting this job was having to go to Bedfordshire for three months' training. I really enjoyed this break away from the city, and on my return, I stayed with the firm for the remainder of my working life.

I cannot help comparing the Scotland Road I knew and loved in my early years to the way it is now. It was once such a thriving, busy road, bustling with people. Of the many shops, I remember Gordons, where I had to take the ration books, the Co-op, Hayes the cooked meat shop, the indoor market by Clarkson's and Hilliards homemade bread and cake shop, to name but a few. There were literally dozens of pubs, almost one on every corner; the women did not have to go far to the shops and the men for their pints. All this added to the character of the neighbourhood and sadly parts of the road are now only a shadow of what they once were.

Thankfully, people like myself still have their memories of a once vibrant and vital part of the city; it is these memories that I like to share with the many children who attend our history sessions in the at the Albert Dock.

MACHINES
TO BE
STARTED AND STOPPED BY
ATTENDANTS ONLY.

TO PREVENT DAMAGE TO
HYDROS (WRINGERS), THESE
MACHINES ARE TO BE
FILLED ALL ROUND
BEFORE BEING STARTED.

Ann Roberts – Born 1937

I was born on the 3 September 1937 – two years exactly before the start of the Second Word War – the youngest of four children: Douglas who was seventeen, Gwen thirteen, and Mary who had died aged nine months. Mary, who was born in 1918, was my mother's first child and her death was never spoken of, except to say that it was God's will.

I do not remember the start of the war, but in May 1941 our house was hit by a land-mine. I can clearly recall the deafening noise, overlaid with the high-pitched sounds of glass cracking and shattering, as the windows were blasted out of their frames. Then the clouds of choking dust and the devastation which was revealed as the dust gradually settled. At the time of the blast, I was lying on a mattress on the cellar floor with two of our neighbour's children, where we had been put for safety during the air-raid. After the bombing, water immediately began to pour down the cellar steps. We thought it so funny as my dad came slipping and sliding down the stairs to check that we were safe.

The house was so badly damaged that we could no longer live there. We moved around the corner and I remember sitting on the back of the wagon with the furniture. We moved into a two up, two down house on the site where the Royal Liverpool Hospital now stands. The pub next door to the Bridewell on the opposite side of Prescot Street was the Blue Ball, where, a few years later, many Liverpudlians made a name for themselves as country and western singers. Around that area, all the houses were different, some were large with attics and cellars, some small; two up, two down. There were even some of the old courts, left over from the 1800s; dark, dank, dreary places, totally unfit for people to live in.

I was a happy child, with a grandad and a grandma and a 'nin' (another grandmother), living close by; an extended family which was the norm in those days. A highlight of my early years was when a doll's house arrived for me by post. My brother Doug and a German prisoner-of-war had made it for me. Later, a miniature three-piece suite also arrived, laboriously fashioned out of fruit seeds and pips. Doug also sent his sweet ration to me, in a small dark green tin.

My dad worked for William Littles and James Newton, shipping

The wash-house not only provided a useful service, it was also a meeting place where women could find advice and support and also exchange the latest gossip.

The Liverpool Overhead Railway, or 'Dockers' Umbrella', was a wonderful way of seeing the docks and the river. As a child, Ann's father would occasionally take her to work with him on the railway and her nose would be pressed up against the window all the way.

merchants, and on occasions he would take me to work with him and we would travel on the Liverpool Overhead Railway, passing all the docks from north to south. My nose would be pressed up against the window as I took in all the different sights and sounds. My dad drove a wagon and we went on many trips to Wales, delivering ships' hardware. Going under the Mersey Tunnel was always a wonder to me – all that water above our heads. Travelling was always a bit of a novelty and I used to long for the tramride we took each spring to Woolton Woods to see the bluebells. The conductor would show us to our seats – chair-like at the front and long benches at the rear – and then punch our tickets, which we thought was great fun. It was also part of the fun to watch the driver change the cable over from the line above to go back into town.

Real life hit me with a bang when I was six and I contracted diphtheria; a serious, life-threatening disease which has thankfully now died out due to mass vaccination. I was nursed in an isolation ward in the John Bagot Hospital in Netherfield Road. Isolation really did mean isolation in those days and I did not see any of my family again for four long months. For most of that time I was confined to bed in a long ward in which a never-ending stream of doctors, nurses and cleaners rushed about – all of them bossy. While I was still very poorly I was fed with a cup which had a spout just like a teapot and had a peculiar smell – the whole process took a very long time.

Once I soiled the bed and was told off very severely for it, but no one had heard me calling for a bedpan as my voice was so weak. As the nurse changed my sheets and pyjamas, tutting and sighing all the while, all eyes seemed to be staring at me down the entire length of the ward and I felt humiliated and ashamed. As I buried my face beneath the sheets, I longed to go home.

Towards the end of my stay I was allowed to eat at a big table in the ward with the other children and as we grew stronger we began to sing and I learnt the words to *If You Were the Only Girl in the World*. I remember the relief I felt on the day I was finally let out and being brought home in a car (how posh!) with my dad's best friend and my mam. Great joy to be back at home with mum and dad and I was really cosseted after that; not allowed out to play out with other children and had to have goose grease rubbed into my chest while I was being bathed in front of the fire. Being the youngest, I was always made a great fuss of by the rest of the family and I remember having my photograph taken at Jeromes in London Road in my first communion day finery and enjoying being the centre of attention.

Ours was a close community and communal celebrations marked every major event in our lives: VE and VJ Day, the Queen's Coronation in 1953 and times of football fever. VE Day was wonderful – everybody seemed so happy. The whole street had been decorated in red, white and blue, with bunting zigzaging across the street from house to house and the kerbstones all painted in alternate colours. All the women had got together to make garlands of flowers out of crêpe paper, which they used to decorate each other's doorways. Tables and chairs were placed in a line down the middle of the street and everyone had to bring a plate, cup and spoon. Each house would provide as much food and drink as they could afford and it would be shared with everyone else. We played games, danced and held competitions – I received a bar of chocolate for singing on top of the air-raid shelter.

Alas! These happy times were punctuated by times of extreme sadness and my security and contentment were not to last. The first tragedy struck when my mother contracted TB and we all had to watch helplessly as it gradually sapped away all her life and strength. Finally, in 1947, when I was only nine years old, my mother passed away, aged forty-four. It was awful and her death left a huge gap in my life, a terrible, aching loneliness. The day of her funeral was one of the most painful in my life and the slow, mournful car journey to Yewtree Cemetery seemed interminable, even though it was actually quite near to where we lived. She was buried in the grave of her sister, Mary, who had died at the age of twenty-four, having suffered from heart problems. The grave had a beautiful headstone of an angel with wide-spread wings. Sadly the angel has been destroyed by today's vandals who seem to have no respect for the dead.

After her death, I worked in the house as much as I could to help my dad and would go for the accumulator for the wireless and run any other errands for him. My dad was a very talented man musically, and could play any instrument. When I look back at him in my mind's eye, I always picture him singing. Tragically, in 1950, he suffered a massive stroke. He was in a coma for two weeks before he too died, when he was just fifty years old. His death was the worst thing that could have happened to me – such a great loss – my world seemed to be falling apart. Looking back, I was fortunate that I had a family to look after me and was not put in an orphanage or shipped out to Australia, New Zealand or Canada, like so many hapless orphans at the time, many of whom were placed with families who treated them like servants, or abused and mistreated them.

Ann in 1946, shortly before her life was to be turned upside-down, firstly by the death of her mother in 1947, and then her father, in 1950.

Remember When ...

Death

- White reins were used on the horses pulling the hearse if the deceased was under twenty-one years of age.

- People in mourning could not always afford the traditional black clothing, so instead, a black band, or diamond, was sewn onto the sleeve of their coat.

- Shops selling mantles (coats) charged top prices for 'mourning' clothes, possibly because of the insurance money.

- During the period when the corpse was lying at home, all the mirrors in the house were covered up.

My father was buried with his family at Ford Cemetery, which unlike Yewtree, really was a long way away from the house. I remember the respect shown by our neighbours as they lined both sides of the street, all along the route, for his funeral, the women blessing themselves and the men doffing their caps as the funeral car passed. With my mother's funeral still a recent memory, the journey to the cemetery was a great sorrow for everyone. Funeral cortèges always proceeded at a very slow pace in those days, much more in keeping with the dignity and solemnity of the occasion than today's hearses which seemingly cannot get to the cemetery quickly enough.

So, at twelve, I was an orphan and the world for me had become a very different and altogether more frightening place. My sister Gwen gained the tenancy of my father's house in West Street, Liverpool 7 and she looked after me. After she married the following Christmas, I continued to live with her and her husband. They received ten shillings and sixpence allowance for my upkeep.

Our next door neighbours, Jane and Massley Jilofsky, were Jewish, and were kindness itself to me. After my dad's death they helped me out by paying me to clean their house for them every Friday. I set the fire, cleaned the brass candlesticks and laid the table with a clean white tablecloth over a dark green chenille one. On their Sabbath they were not allowed to do any work at all, so I shopped for them at the kosher butchers in Pembroke Place, which is still there today, facing the old Royal Hospital, built November 1889. I liked to watch the 'bobby' on point duty in his little white box, in the middle of the road, controlling the traffic in eight directions. As well as the Jewish butchers, there was the other Jewish shop in Furclough Lane, where, each Sunday, we bought our bagels to eat with salt fish. The floor was covered in sawdust, shuffled into endless different patterns by the trample of customers' feet. I loved to gaze at the rows of jars containing unfamiliar foreign food like herrings, sauerkraut, dill cucumber, salt beef and rye bread. The shopkeeper and many of his customers all spoke with the same funny accent. There was also a shop at either end of West Street where we lived.

As well as all the shops, the area was full of different institutions. There was the sandstone-built ragged school run by the Sisters of Mercy in the 1800s for the poor of the parish, now an ordinary primary school, and the convent next door where you could buy medicine made by the nuns for a shilling a bottle. The Sisters of Mercy, founded in 1817 in Falkner Street, Mount Pleasant, wore stark black habits, with a stiff white wimple biting painfully into their faces and seemed to be very hard workers in the community. They also went round collecting money from houses and shops.

The wash-house in Minshul Street was another familiar landmark, a place where women not only did their weekly washing, but caught up with all the neighbourhood gossip at the same time. Sometimes, for a small charge, women did other people's laundry too, the few extra coppers helping them to make ends meet. These women would leave the wash-house proudly carrying a large, round bundle on their heads, wearing big, business-like boots and a shawl round their shoulders.

The streets were much more 'lived in' in those days – there was always something going on. Early in the morning housewives would be out,

scrubbing their steps with a 'donkey' stone. It was a point of honour to keep the back and the front of your house clean, which meant that the streets looked much more cared for than they do today. But it was yet another task which required a lot of hard, physical work for the women of the household, giving them swollen arthritic knees and red, calloused hands. Little traffic went up and down the residential streets, just the brown and yellow bread van of Prices the Baker, the ragman, or the odd car, or horse and cart, so children could play in relative safety.

Growing up in Liverpool during the war years, we had plenty of picture houses near our home. I lived just a few minutes' walk from the Majestic near London Road, a really wonderful place from which to escape the real world. The cinema had marble walls, huge tiles on the floor, carpets everywhere, wonderful lights and plush seating. The lavish stage boasted ruched net curtains behind velvet drapes, which, when they opened up, had different coloured spotlights playing upon them. What a sight to behold! The paintwork was in rich, classical colours, reminiscent of old religious paintings; gold, amber, blue, green, red and purple.

The Hippodrome was another local cinema, but this had none of the opulence of the Majestic. Here you had to climb up stone steps to sit in the cheapest seats – long wooden forms – so uncomfortable. It was a real let down after the Majestic. The Lytton, in Everton Road, was another cheap place, a 'flea pit' where the attendants regularly sprayed the audience with a 'Flit' gun. You could get into the Saturday matinee using clean jam jars instead of money. The cinema was the focus for our young dreams; it shaped our attitudes and taste for things, even if many of the luxuries were way beyond our means. We also gained a taste for good books and classical music.

I remember going with our teacher to watch *Oliver Twist,* an adaptation

of Charles Dickens' classic novel, when I was fourteen. Far from detracting from the story, the black and white film really lent atmosphere to the dark plot. In the opening scene, a heavily pregnant young girl was struggling across the bleak moors to reach the workhouse. I was an orphan myself, and somehow this scene played on my mind for a very long time; her treatment seemed so heartless and cruel.

Buskers would entertain the people queueing outside the cinema; people were prepared to wait for hours to get in, especially if it was an epic film. I saw my first zither played outside the Majestic, and a performer called Hughie used to be tied up with chains, then locked in a canvas bag. We held our breath as he struggled wildly inside the bag. Every time he would take ages to escape, but he always managed it in the end.

The glamorous films made us long to be film stars, singing and dancing our way through life, enjoying sleek cars, luxurious restaurants and elegant clothes. If only! They always featured comfortable homes with telephones, lace curtains, carpets, fridges and drinks cupboards, and, of course, inside toilets and bathrooms. Heaven! We went home to a tin bath and an outside loo! Some people went to the cinema to keep warm, especially the very poor whose homes had no floor covering, or comfort of any kind. They could also keep up with current events with the Pathé newsreel, as not everyone had a wireless. The cinema helped us to overcome the problems of the 1930s Depression and the horrors of war. We could forget them for a while, and wallow instead in the artificial glamour of Hollywood.

I left school in 1952, aged fifteen years. I wanted to be a seamstress, but the pay was too low – one pound seven shillings a week – compared to factory work. So I began work as a flat machinist in the Lybro for more money. It was piecework. I handed my pay packet over to my sister for my keep and was given one pound for clothes, fares, entertainment, dancing, skating and make-up. Fortunately, boyfriends paid for you when you went out in those days, so I managed quite well. I loved to go dancing, especially when rock and roll came along.

My sister had a baby boy in 1952, and a year later grandad died. Then Gwen had another son a year later. Things seemed to be improving and rationing, which had gradually been phased out since the end of the war, finally ended. My sister was at home all the time, looking after the children, and I loved her two boys like brothers, however, I eventually felt in the way, and I decided it was time to move on. The flat I moved to cost me one pound seventeen shillings a week. It was only a bedsit with an upstairs kitchen, but I loved having my independence, until I discovered that the house was overrun with cockroaches. I left in fright.

My next move was to a one-roomed flat in Fairfield, where I paid the same rent. There was a bath with hot water from a geyser which cost five pence every time you used it. I had to share the bath and a toilet with ten other people. Having to find enough pennies for the gas fire and cooker became quite a drain on my purse, because I still had to buy food and clothes, and I discovered the downside of independence. I had a new boyfriend at this time, Robert, and he paid for me when we went out but I still needed more money and I managed to get a job in the Meccano as a printer. I earned good money doing twelve-hour shifts, three days a week. My financial situation improved again when I once more moved jobs to work at the Automatic Telephone Company, where the wages were even better.

Robert and I were married in 1958 and we continued to live in my flat for another year, after which we shared a house with friends for a while. Wages for men at that time were about three pounds ten shillings a week, and I was also working.

Our first daughter was born in 1960, and my sister cared for her so that I could carry on working. We were saving hard to buy our own house, which we eventually bought for five hundred pounds. The situation in the country was still gradually improving; there were plenty of jobs and our own situation seemed to be improving as well; I soon became pregnant again and we both had good jobs. Then disaster struck when my second daughter died. Not only were we devastated emotionally, but we also had to face the cost of her funeral, which stretched us beyond our means. We received a grant of seven pounds from the Government, but she had to be buried in the grave of another family. Life had to go on, and we pulled together.

My son was born in 1963 and I gave up my full time job and cleaned pubs instead so that my children were not with my sister for too long. We were happy enough with our lot, and ready to face whatever came our way. Robert and I have now been married for forty-three years and we have a son and daughter and eight grandchildren.

The Meccano factory provided employment for large numbers of people, mainly women.

BOVRIL CARAMELS

PREVENTS THAT SINKING FEELING

Deryn Jones – Born 1937

I was born in 1937, the eldest of four girls. We lived with my grandparents and an uncle in their corporation house in Norris Green. It was a three-bedroom parlour house, with a bathroom and toilet upstairs; we also had a garden. Compared to the conditions some people were living in at the time, we were very fortunate.

When my grandmother died, my Mum continued to look after her father and brother, as well as caring for her own family. She had had three children in three and a half years, and to add to her problems, I was asthmatic. My earliest memories are of her working hard all day running the home, and then having to sit up all night with me when I was ill.

While I was still a toddler the war started and my uncle went into the Army. There was now only my dad's small wage coming in, and money was very tight. One painful memory was of being ill and my mum pacing up and down in the kitchen, waiting for my dad to come home, to ask him if she should send for the doctor, or buy food for the tea, she could not afford both. This was the time before the National Health Service. During the war I remember going into the air-raid shelter in the garden, which was a totally unsuitable place for a severely asthmatic child, being both cold and damp. But, of course, we had no choice. One night we came out of the shelter to find that a landmine had dropped close by on the Railway Bridge at Broadway.

The treatment for the type of asthma I suffered from was Ephedrine. Inhalers had yet to be invented. If they had have been I might have been able to stay on at my local school but, as it was, I had to go to Fazackerly open-air school and even then I was often absent when my condition worsened. I was picked up and taken there by bus, which made me feel different from other children, and some of them called me names. It was a nice school, but I was not happy there. I would much rather have gone to the local school with my sisters and friends from our area. It seemed to isolate me from them. My constant wheezing and breathlessness also meant that I could not join in many of the other children's games. Because I was unhappy and did not settle well into my school, and was frequently absent I did not do well in my schoolwork. The only good thing about my schooldays was that I met and

Shop windows had no security shutters and had beautiful displays, such as the lovely dressed dolls in the Singer sewing machine shops, and the decorated Easter eggs in the sweet shops at Easter. Shop windows were lit up all night long before the war.

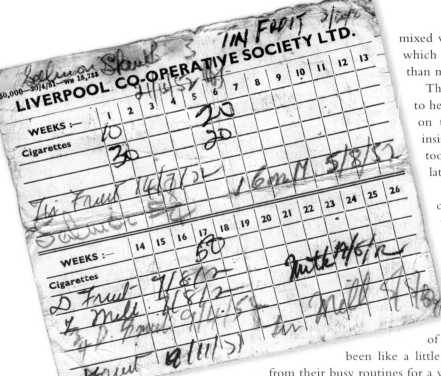

Many people shopped exclusively at the Co-op because of the dividend or 'divi'.

mixed with children from other areas in Liverpool, which probably gave me a slightly broader outlook than my peers.

The doctor recommended fresh air and exercise to help my condition, so my father would take me on the ferryboat, on the top deck, where he insisted I do all my breathing exercises. I was not too happy about this at the time, but realised later that it was all for my own good.

Although I was unhappy at school, this certainly was not the case at home. My mum was always singing, and she always welcomed our friends into the house. No amount of noise or activity of children playing seemed to upset her. I cannot ever remember her telling us off. It was not just children who were welcome in our house; many of the neighbours would also pop in for a cup of tea and a chat. Looking back, it must have been like a little haven for these women, they could escape from their busy routines for a while and talk to others who shared the same problems and anxieties.

My mum's kindness was often repaid; neighbours would find time to visit me when I was off school ill, and they would play cards and other games with me. It was a neighbour who looked after us the day my mum was having her last baby, my sister Pat.

In those days our area in Norris Green was a good, safe place to live, we had a few local shops and we were close to Broadway, which was a busy shopping area. My mum would go there every day. It was not just the shopping she went for, it was also a chance for her to meet up with people she knew. Most of our shopping was done at the Co-op, because of the 'divi' (dividend) which was paid out twice a year; my mum always tried to save hers up for Christmas. We had three Co-op stores in the area, Broadway, Stopgate Lane and Langford Avenue.

There were also three local picture houses; the Regal in Broadway, (where I saw my first film, *Pinocchio*), the Victoria in Cherry Lane, and the Clubmoor. Going to the pictures was always a treat. I remember staying with my aunt in Liscard and she took me to see *Showboat*, which has remained my all time favourite film. While enjoying the film, I also kept hoping that she would buy me an ice cream.

Every year there was a fun fair at Walton Hall Park and, as the day of the fair drew near, we would collect jam jars from all the neighbours and take them to Nelsons Jam factory in Long Lane, where they would give us a penny for two jars. We would rush off to the fair to spend our 'fortune'. I loved the swing boats best, and we always tried to win an ornament for my mum's sideboard.

We were luckier than most children when it came to holidays, because my dad originally came from Llangollen and most of his family still lived there.

One of Deryn's local picture houses was the Regal, Broadway. It was here that she saw her very first film, 'Pinocchio'.

This picture shows the interior of the Victoria, Cherry Lane; another of Deryn's favourite haunts.

He would take my sister Nina and me to stay with them. It was not really much of a holiday for him, because he worked on the canal barges while we enjoyed ourselves, but he liked seeing his family.

I left school when I was fifteen, and my first job was at the Singer Sewing Machines shop in London Road. I did not stay there long because I found it too quiet. There was however some excitement one day when the Andrew Sisters came in, they were appearing at the Empire theatre. They wanted someone to put buttonholes in their jackets. My boss told me to take them to Day's sewing factory, which I did, and they gave me a half crown tip, I have never forgotten the incident, and no, I did not keep the half crown as a souvenir, I spent it.

My next job was in Trueform shoe shop, which was also in London Road. I loved working there and was often tempted to buy shoes which I could get at cut price. I remember my dad bringing my little sister Pat into the shop, to buy her a pair of the white buckskin boots that were so very popular in the 1950s. I look upon this period of my life as one of the best times for my mum and myself. With my sisters at school, she was free to meet me at lunchtime every Thursday at TJ Hughes, just the two of us. After having some lunch, we would walk around the store and perhaps buy some small item for the house. These times were special for me and I know my mum enjoyed them too.

I left Trueform to work in Goldrei Fucard, in Brookfield drive, a firm making cake decorations, including the bride and groom figures for wedding cakes. Whether or not they had smiles on their faces depended on what sort of mood we were in at the time!

My teenage years were very happy. I was in a formation dancing team aVaughan's dance school, where I went four nights a week. I also loved going to the pictures. Quite often my friends and I would go straight from the first house at the pictures, to the dance. The theatre was another favourite pastime. Stars like Guy Mitchell, Frankie Lane, Nat King Cole and Johnny Rae, all appeared at the Empire. I went to see them all. Guy Mitchell was my favourite and after going around to the stage door and seeing him in person, I joined his fan club.

My first holiday without my family was spent in Towyn, in North Wales, when myself and five other girls stayed in a converted railway carriage for a week. We had a wonderful time. There was no flying out to the sun for us in those days, that came much later.

In 1957 I started a new job in AC Delco, in Kirkby, making parts for cars. The factory was only partly built and the room I worked in only had three walls. The other wall was just a sheet of tarpaulin. It was bitterly cold in winter, and the general working conditions were awful. There were no washing facilities, even though we were working all day long with grease and oil. It was assembly line work, which meant that we had to be relieved by another worker before we could go to the toilet. Conditions eventually did improve somewhat, but only because of the efforts of the trade union.

Although ninety per cent of the workforce was made up of women, it was not until 1992 that the first forewoman was appointed. Working with so many women meant that there would always be a celebration of some sort going on: engagements, weddings, christenings etc, which made the job much more enjoyable. We also had various saving schemes operating: perm clubs, hamper clubs and a great favourite, the money club. I remember when it was my turn to be paid out from the money club, I had been planning what I would spend the money on for weeks. I rushed off to town and headed straight for C & A Modes, where I bought myself a coat, two dresses and two taffeta skirts, complete with underskirts – all for £25! I could not wait to get home and try them all on again.

Conditions at Delco could not have been too bad, because I spent the rest of my working life there. The factory was a community in its own right; everybody knew everybody else and strong friendships were formed amongst the workers. I made many good friends there; friends that I still have after forty-five years.

I never married, through choice; being tied down with children did not appeal to me. However, I do have many nieces and nephews whom I love dearly, and who are an important part of my life. I also get great pleasure from meeting the hundreds of schoolchildren who come to our History for Schools sessions at the Albert Dock.

Nina Barr – Born 1939

I was born in 1939, the second daughter of four girls. We lived in a council house in Norris Green. It had three bedrooms, a parlour, living room, back kitchen, bathroom and toilet, and a large garden back and front. Being so young, I do not remember much about the war, but I clearly remember the Anderson air-raid shelter in the back garden, which we played in long after the war. It was made of corrugated galvanised steel and was erected in a pit about three or four feet deep. Inside, it was always cold and damp and very dark as it had no windows.

I also remember going to the shops for mum and having to take the ration books with us. Rationing continued after the war and gradually came to an end in the 1950s. Another memory that stays in my mind is of our teacher giving us all a tin of dried egg and a tin of cocoa. Whether this was a charitable donation from some local source, or was provided by the Government, I am not sure, but dried egg was very popular, especially with children, and would have been much appreciated as a gift by poor families.

My family was quite poor. My dad did have a job as an engineer, but it was not very well paid and mum had to struggle to make ends meet. My sisters and I used to go round the streets pushing a big old pram, asking the neighbours for empty jam jars. After collecting as many as we could, we would take them home and wash them and then take them along to Hartley's jam factory, where they would give us a penny for every four jars. The proceeds would be spent at the local rummage sale to buy socks and knickers, which helped mum out a little.

I left school when I was fifteen and went to work in a factory which made cake decorations, such items as bride and groom figures and flowers and pedestals to separate cake tiers. During the time I was working there, another young girl, a friend of my sister's who was about nineteen years old, became pregnant. In those days, such a thing was a huge scandal and the poor girl would be virtually ostracised by the community. This particular girl was the talk of the factory and few people would have anything to do with her. But we stood by her and she would have her lunch with us. Some time later she married her boyfriend, so the baby was born in wedlock. But, sadly, it was to be their only child, because he was soon killed in a motorbike accident when

The Tower Ballroom in New Brighton is remembered with affection by many of the women as a place where they regularly used to go dancing.

Nina, aged sixteen, wearing the fashion of the day.

he was just eighteen. I loved my job and stayed with the same firm for about ten years, even though my wages were very poor. My two sisters worked in a factory making car parts and they earned about twice as much as me.

When I was about seventeen or eighteen, my friends and I used to go dancing. We would spend ages getting ready for the dance and after all the trouble we took, we would then spend the whole night standing around waiting for a lad to ask us to dance. In those days girls would never dance together, not until the Jive came in, that is, then you could get up and dance with your friends. This was a big step forward for us. It knocked the stuffing out of the lads and stopped them strutting about thinking how great they were.

When my friend was getting married she asked me to 'stand' for her on her wedding day. The wedding was a rather sad, low-key affair, as she came from a large family who could not afford a big wedding. So there was only the bride and groom and the groom's brother who was the best man, and myself. Our footsteps echoed gloomily as we walked down the aisle of the empty church – there were no other guests. When it was all over we went to the local shops and bought ten cigarettes, then we went to the bride's home, where her mum had a meal ready for us.

I was twenty-four when I got married. We had saved hard for two years and the wedding cost us about eight hundred pounds. We booked the Co-op hall for the reception and had to bring all the drink in ourselves and arrange for someone to serve it from a table, which we used as the bar. We went to the Isle of Man for our honeymoon and we thought we were 'dead posh' flying for the first time.

We had four children – two girls and two boys. My first baby was born in 1964. When I first discovered that I was pregnant my doctor arranged an appointment for me at the antenatal clinic at Mill Road Hospital. On my first visit I had a blood test and was then given a number and had to wait with a long line of women for my number to appear on the indicator. Then it was my turn to go into a cubicle where a doctor examined me. I found this system very impersonal, with every patient being addressed as 'Mrs', whether they were married or not. This must have upset the single mothers and made them feel patronised.

The time finally arrived when I was in labour and my husband took me to the hospital, where a nurse met us at the door. He was promptly sent home with instructions to telephone the hospital later. I was very frightened – I just did not know what to expect. However, when the pains grew really bad, a nurse came and sat with me and showed me how to relax my body, starting with my toes. I found this a great help. I was also given gas and air to ease the pain. After six hours in labour, I gave birth to a baby girl with the help of forceps. I stayed in hospital for a week, during which time I was shown how to breastfeed my baby and to bath her. She was born with a harelip. Previously a child like this would have had to wait until she was fully grown before they would operate and even then the results were often poor. But we were lucky, they had just started doing this kind of operation while the babies were very young. She was only three months old when she was operated on and when she came out of hospital it was just like a miracle, her little mouth was perfect.

Two years later I had a little boy and two years after that, another girl. The routine at Mill Road remained the same. Then, twelve years later, I became pregnant again and this time I attended Fazackerly Hospital. I just could not believe the difference; everything was so much more relaxed. There was a lounge with comfortable chairs where you could sit with your visitors, and there was also a tea and coffee machine. The general atmosphere was so much friendlier, with every woman being called by her first name. I gave birth to my fourth baby, another boy, and I was only in hospital for a day. I was delighted; we now had two boys and two girls, our family was complete.

Our children were all fine and healthy and we now have grandchildren. Now that I am in my early sixties, I have time for myself at last, and I occupy much of it with the Women's History Group, and enjoy every minute of it.

Nina's mother would have used a mask such as this for her when she was a baby. The baby had to be put into the mask headfirst, with just its legs exposed and it was tied securely with tapes around the baby's waist. There was a small hand pump at the side which the mother worked to give the baby air.

Anne Baker – Born 1950

I was born in 1950 in the Parish of St Albans, in the north end of the city, in what is now called the Vauxhall area. It was commonly referred to by the locals as 'over the bridge'. The bridge in question, or three bridges to be exact, were the thoroughfares of Boundary Street, Athol Street and Lightbody Street, which were the three access roads into the dockland area where I grew up. The bridges cross over the Leeds/Liverpool canal, which has always been the unofficial boundary line that children from either side were not allowed to cross, unless accompanied by an adult. Outsiders often called the area 'the village' or 'little Ireland'. The village, because we were an isolated community, and little Ireland, because the majority of the people, including my family, were descendants of the Irish immigrants who flocked to Liverpool during the Irish Potato Famine.

The whole area was purely Catholic. Protestants were not tolerated at any cost. On one occasion a new family moved into the lock-keeper's house. The father worked on the lock and the mother found herself a job as an assistant in the local corner shop. She was a perfectly pleasant woman, who tried her best to fit into our community with her family. But she did not stand a chance, because word soon got around that the family was Protestant and the local people started to boycott the shop where she worked. The argument was that the shop owner should have given the job to one of his own (a Catholic). The family was completely ostracised. The neighbours reprimanded anyone seen talking to them, or going into the shop. This happened to my mother when she was once seen coming out of the shop. She was very upset by it, and felt it was terrible the way that family was being treated. But religious bigotry in Liverpool was rife both in the community and in the workplace. I remember my dad saying that even though we lived in an area surrounded by factories, no Catholic could get a job. Times were hard if you were a Catholic. Some men applying for work would say they were Protestant, but would soon be shown the door once it was known where they lived.

But thank goodness times have changed. In the early 1960s, when the whole area was rebuilt, the Council, in its wisdom, decided to demolish the whole 'over the bridge' area and start again from scratch. Many new families

A typical terraced street of the 1960s with just one parked car – very different from today's congested streets.

Anne as a young girl.

were brought into the area, including the dreaded Protestants. After a while, commonsense prevailed and religious bigotry from both sides soon disappeared and friendships were formed across the religious divide. You used to often hear the phrase, "You're alright, considering you're a Catholic/Protestant!" said jokingly between people in those days.

The Welsh people who came to Liverpool to settle and work first built the area called 'over the bridge'. Then, as they became more affluent, they moved out into better homes in better areas, but left behind the street names which are all named after Welsh towns. My family lived in Snowdon Street, in a two-up-two-down terraced house. There was no bathroom and no kitchen. My mother cooked on the small black range and used an enamel bowl as her sink. Bath night was the usual tin bath with water drawn from a tap in the backyard that was attached to the toilet wall. I am the middle child of five children, with a brother and sister older, and a brother and sister younger than me. Like many people growing up in the fifties, we were very poor, but poverty had no meaning to us as children. We had no television to show us what we were missing in the material world; we were happy and carefree.

Even though I was born after the war had come to an end, it still cast its long shadow over my childhood. My mother had worked in a munitions factory during the war and had lost her hearing when an explosion at work burst both her eardrums, and my dad had been seriously injured twice during his time in the Army, once when a bullet narrowly missed his heart. I had also lost my paternal grandmother during the war, killed by a bomb as she was trying to get to the air-raid shelter. Both my parents' post-war years were scarred by these events. And then there was the area itself, with its docks and railways which had made it a prime target for the German bombers, one of the most heavily bombed places in Liverpool.

My childhood was spent playing on the numerous bombsites that littered the whole area. The bricks and pieces of wood became our toys. We girls would create elaborate houses and shops, two bricks high, (we were not allowed to build higher than that for safety reasons), which we also furnished with materials scavenged from the rubble. When we had finished building, we would sit in our handmade chairs at our handmade tables eating jam butties and drinking cups of water pretending we were having a party. The boys played cowboys and indians and other games using the mounds of bricks as make-believe mountains. The bomb craters were turned into dens. These and many other games were created out of our giant Lego set. Our only limitation was our imagination.

There is one place that the locals called the 'Dead House'. It was an old school dinner centre built under the railway arches at the bottom of Boundary Street. During the war it had unwisely been used as an air-raid shelter. The inevitable happened. The railway, being a prime target, received a direct hit and many people sheltering beneath the arches were killed. From that time on the place was said to be haunted. It certainly did have a creepy atmosphere about it and although it could be used as a short cut, even grown men avoided going near it. You always felt that you were being watched or followed.

After the war my dad went to work in Douglas's, a local foundry, as a blacksmith striker. It was hard, dirty, heavy work, but he stayed there until he retired in bad health at the age of sixty-two. As we children got older, my mother also went out to work as an office cleaner, to help out with the family budget.

When I was six my mother was told that I had asthma, or as they called it then – a weak chest. I was sent to Fazackerly Open-Air School, for children with health problems. I spent many happy years in that school. I left when I was fifteen and started my working life at Littlewoods Pools, in Walton Hall Avenue.

My childhood memories have certainly been stimulated since I joined the Women's History Group. Listening to the other women's wartime stories and getting involved in the workshops has been a real education to me. It has brought home to me the true horror of the wartime experiences, not only of the Armed Forces, but of the ordinary civilians as well. I first heard about this group when I was doing the Second Chance to Learn course at Liverpool Community College – little did I know then that I would soon become an active member. At first I thought that I would never be able to take any active part in the workshops. But each week I was drawn back, fascinated by what was going on. I was encouraged to join in, but I was far too self-conscious. But gradually, with a lot of patience from the other members, I found the confidence to take part.

Conclusion

We hope our book has sparked off memories in our older readers. Perhaps they can identify with the tin bath and going 'the messages' to the corner shop. Perhaps they had their own 'Mr Jones' who called to check if they were really entitled to their few shilling's relief money. Maybe they will remember the pawnshop, and getting a few groceries from the corner shop on 'tick', and shopping in Great Homer Street on a Saturday night for cheap food in the hungry 1930s. This world-wide depression would fit them well for the horrors of the war.

Some younger people too will recall the evacuation, when children were wrenched from their homes and taken to a strange town or village, to live with people who did not always welcome them. The rationing, which made meals so boring; spuds, spuds, more spuds and carrots. The endless food queues and the magic of getting hold of a few oranges. Mind you, before the war, food was rationed by price, so the working classes were already well used to deprivation. Then the Blitz. Looking back, it is hard to believe we suffered all those nights of sheer terror. In no way can we adequately describe the horror of those times when thousands of people were killed, maimed and left homeless.

Although we do our best to relate to the classes of children what life in the 1930s was really like, we cannot expect them to fully understand the experience. Of course, they can read about it in books, or watch war scenes on television, but we were there, we are living witnesses.

We describe how we felt, and in doing so, sometimes bring tears to their eyes, but we also make them laugh and always send them on their way with a song.

We teach the children Social History, and in the process, we have fun together. We hope we succeed in bridging the gap between the ages and that our workshops and this book will give them an understanding of the lives we lived – a very different world.